NAVIGATING THE ADAPTIVE ECONOMY

MANAGING BUSINESS RISK AND OPPORTUNITY IN A CHANGING CLIMATE

DAVID MCEWEN

Published by

Adaptive Capability Pty Ltd

L9, 580 George St

Sydney, NSW 2000

Australia

www.adaptivecapability.com

ISBN: 978-0-9946430-0-1

For more information please visit www.AdaptiveEconomyBook.com

Disclaimer

The author does not specifically advocate any of the companies or business ideas presented in this book. In particular, it is not intended that the ideas herein necessarily represent environmentally sound options. People considering exploiting any of the potential products and services should undertake their own research and due diligence, including seeking independent, qualified advice as to how the various impacts of climate change, including the associated regulatory and societal responses might affect their business plans. The contents of this book do not constitute investment advice and no liability is taken for any loss or damage arising.

Contents

Forward

The purpose of this book is to provide a tool kit for business owners and executives to shape strategic climate change action plans in ways that preserve and enhance business value while also delivering environmental benefits.

The subject matter is focused on the business opportunities and risks of adapting to a changing climate and the associated global response. It identifies a range of sectors whose products and services are either at risk or could benefit from these changes. It points out numerous areas where innovation will be needed to develop new products and services to meet changing needs.

This book is not about developing a corporate sustainability plan or making marginal energy efficiency improvements, though they are useful initiatives in their own right.

Now is our pivotal moment

This century, everything changes. The high speed growth trajectory the world has been on since the start of the industrial revolution is almost over. As our populations and environmental impact have multiplied, we now find ourselves occupying a planet that is straining to accommodate our insatiable appetite for food, water, energy, resources and things.

While technological innovation has allowed us to get away with this unsustainable resource consumption in the decades since we outstripped the earth's carrying capacity, we are facing increasing disruptive threats in the form of climate change, polluted air, water and soils, depleted fisheries, forests and other critical eco-systems.

Soon, within a handful of decades or less, everything must peak: peak fossil fuel dependence, peak population, peak pollution, peak per-capita consumption, peak greenhouse gas emissions. Otherwise – just as happens in nature and has happened before in human history – a population that grows and lives beyond its means faces collapse.

Declining fertility rates in developing and developed countries suggest that the global population will stabilise at about 10 billion around 2050. That reduction in demand growth will eventually have staggering impacts in economies that are built on the premise of continuous expansion. However, there will still be billions of people hoping to claw their way out of poverty and achieve the consumptive capacity of the middle class, meaning more food (including more complex, protein based foods), more energy and more stuff – from disposable nappies to handbags to TVs and tablets – will be demanded.

In many countries the average age of the population is increasing, with a massive demographic shift expected in the proportion of workers compared with retirees. This will also affect growth and spending patterns.

Meanwhile we have used our planet as a giant chemistry experiment, changing the composition of atmospheric gases, soils, fresh water systems and oceans in ways that are now material, and with effects that we are only starting to understand. This is repeated in the way we have upset the balance of many ecosystems and made thousands of species extinct through land clearing, wetland draining and poorly managed use of herbicides and pesticides. Millions of years of evolution creating complex food chains and biological balancing systems has been upset in just the last few decades.

In short, the twenty first century is going to be marked by a confluence of changes that will challenge the way of life we are used to. While this book's focus is on the impacts of climate change and how these can be harnessed by companies to reduce risk and create competitive advantage, it is set against the broader background of humanity's influence on its environment and associated demographic, social and technological mega trends.

Introduction
The Debate Is Over

In May 2014, comedian John Oliver, host of HBO's "Last Week Tonight" news satire, demonstrated comprehensively why there is no longer any need for debate about whether climate change is happening (it is), or what's causing it (mostly human activities).[i]

In the clip he starts off by showing a typical climate debate organised by a news or current affairs show, in which a lone scientist is pitted against a climate change denier. In this setting it's all too easy for the scientist to be drowned out by often slick-talking deniers with cherry-picked facts, pseudo-science, sustained attacks on the veracity of key United Nations IPCC[1] findings, or assertions of a conspiracy to undermine our way of life and "send us all back to the Stone Age".

Then Oliver resets the scene and demonstrates how lop-sided that type of debate is, by bringing 97 climate scientists onto the set, surrounding an uncomfortable group of three denialists. While in this case the majority of participants were members of the studio audience dressed in lab coats, the point that deniers are a very, very small minority is well made.

Across several studies including surveys and literature reviews, over 90% of climate scientists[2] agree, with extremely high confidence levels, that human activity is warming the planet.[ii] They agree this warming is being caused predominantly by the burning of fossil fuels (coal, oil and gas) and changes in land use (deforestation and other land clearing). And they agree that the consequences of this warming, even for current generations, could be pretty dire. As Oxford-based researcher Stephen Emmott wrote recently in language uncharacteristically hyperbolic for the scientific community: "personally, I think we're f****d".[iii]

---

1   The United Nations Intergovernmental Panel on Climate Change

2   and depending on the particular study as many as 97%

The UN IPCC is the peak global scientific body regarding climate change, along with the World Meteorological Organization (WMO). Every five to seven years it produces a major report that collates published, peer-reviewed research from thousands of climate scientists and synthesises the data to produce a massive three volume report. Each of the statements and predictions the IPCC makes is caveated in terms of the strength of the available evidence and the estimated probability of it being correct, based on rigorous scientific analysis. Its 2014 summary states that "...warming of the atmosphere and ocean systems is unequivocal" – a particularly strong statement for scientists.

It goes on to say that "...it is extremely likely that human influence has been the dominant cause of observed warming since 1950..."[iv]

So why aren't we rushing to do something about it?

Surely, if the evidence is clear that humans are responsible we can change our behaviours and fix the problem, right? After all, human beings are the most adaptable species on the planet and have survived and thrived in all corners of the globe.

Unfortunately, it's a little bit harder than that, for a number of reasons.

First is the psychology of risk. Climate change is occurring gradually and its impact seems distant or geographically remote. It is much easier to focus on day to day issues like the economy or Ebola outbreaks or fundamentalist terrorism.

Even extreme weather events like Hurricane Sandy have only a temporary and limited effect in galvanising public support to take action on climate change. Malcolm Gladwell explores this phenomenon in his book David and Goliath, using the example of how the confidence of Londoners in World War II, far from being crushed by the German Blitz, was instead enhanced because of the way the majority of people respond to near misses and traumatic events by gaining a sense of resilience and invulnerability.

In fact, the more climate scientists issue doomsday warnings of cities being submerged, crops ruined by searing heat waves, drought and so on, the more impervious many people are becoming. Human history is littered with stories of civilisations collapsing after failing to manage local resources sustainably, such as food, water, timber and fuel. Often there are ample warnings of impending calamity, which nevertheless go unheeded until it's too late, as recounted by scientist Jared Diamond in his book Collapse.

The age of our leaders also affects their risk psychology and consequent policy decisions relating to climate change. Politicians as a group tend to have an average age that is much higher than the population of constituents they represent. The older one is, the less likely one will experience the impacts of climate change first hand. So warnings of future consequences – even in the second half of this century – seem remote, and this flows into policy settings and decision-making that is more near-term focused.

Secondly, **climate change is an international problem** and effective mitigation requires a coordinated international response to reduce anthropogenic greenhouse gas emissions. There is a precedent for this in the form of the Montreal Protocol, which was ratified by most of the world's nations and required relatively rapid curtailment of the use of ozone depleting chlorofluorocarbon (CFC) gases.[3] However, there are factors at play this time around that are actively working against the chances of a global agreement, with many countries waiting for other countries to act, citing concerns they could jeopardise their economies by taking action in isolation.

Another major obstacle to multilateral agreement is that the highest growth in greenhouse gas emissions is coming from rapidly developing economies such as Brazil and India. However, it has been the major Western economies that have benefitted most from the use of the energy released from burning fossil fuels (and amongst other things the emissions associated with higher consumption of meat). Meanwhile the developing world has only fairly recently started emitting greenhouse gases in bulk, as countries have adopted more liberal economies and realised that one of the keys to prosperity is the availability of energy. This has led to alarming sound-bites such as the assertion that China is commissioning a new coal fired power station every week to meet the needs of its emerging upper and middle classes (fortunately China has recently announced measures to arrest this growth and is already the largest investor of renewable energy, though its emissions are still growing).

Understandably, when developed countries have sought a global agreement to reduce greenhouse emissions, many developing countries have argued that since the West has had a 200 year head start and has contributed the bulk of anthropogenic (human caused) emissions to date, it should be getting its own house in order through deep cuts before seeking to impose its will on

---

3   Incidentally, CFCs are also greenhouse gases, though so too are the hydro fluorocarbon (HFC) compounds that have generally replaced CFCs.

developing nations that have not shared the benefits. The contentious topic of funding for developing nations to implement emissions cuts has been another reason that climate talks stalled over the last decade.

Thirdly, unlike the depletion of the ozone layer, which required a relatively narrow set of changes – the substitution of CFCs for non-ozone depleting refrigerants and propellants, which were available at minimum additional cost and required few if any changes to product design or use – mitigation of our GHG emissions requires a **much more fundamental, expensive and challenging transformation**.

Our current economy is – literally – built on oil and other fossil fuels. Consider these facts:[v]

- Around 88% of the world's energy consumption comes from burning fossil fuels.

- Global energy consumption increased by 27% between the 1990s and 2000s (decadal total 1994-2003 vs 2004-2013). Despite the increase in renewables and other non-fossil fuel energy sources, global consumption of fossil fuels has still increased 27% over the last decade, in lockstep with overall energy consumption. Over 96% of vehicles rely on fossil fuels apart from a small fraction using bio fuels and a tiny percentage of electric vehicles.[vi]

- Oil and the byproducts of the process of turning it into petroleum are principal inputs used in over 6,000 products, from fertilisers that are currently critical to food production, to plastics, toys, perfume and soap, insecticide, asphalt, shoe polish and paint.

- 55% of a typical equities-based superannuation fund is made up of companies whose main activity relates to the extraction, distribution and exploitation of fossil fuels.[vii]

In short, conquering our fossil fuel dependence requires wholesale changes to a broad range of critical economic systems including energy, transportation, food production, housing, urban planning, manufacturing and even the services economy.

And that's just the start. In addition to the burning of fossil fuels, another major contributor to global warming is agriculture, forestry and other changes to land use.[viii] According to UN data, deforestation for farming, forestry and other reasons currently results in a net loss of forest cover equivalent to about 5.2 million hectares per annum – an area the size of Costa Rica.[ix] While this rate has decreased over the last couple of decades due to concern about the environmental and longer term economic impacts, the challenge of feeding more people and producing more wood products contributes nearly a third of the world's anthropogenic greenhouse gas emissions. Arresting this impact would take substantial adjustments to our approach to food and timber/pulp production.

Similarly, industrial processes produce a range of greenhouse gases that are independent of energy consumption.

For example, the cement industry is estimated to produce 2-3% of total anthropogenic emissions due to the chemical processes involved in concrete production and usage. That's independent of the energy-related emissions associated with cement production, which are estimated to produce a further 2% of greenhouse emissions.[x] Steel production and other chemical processes produce significant greenhouse gases on top of the emissions associated with the energy used in production.

Fourthly, in countries influenced by right-wing political groups, **faith in the virtues of a market-led economy** and consequent anathema towards perceived "big government" intervention is restricting action. A parade of eminent economists has studied the emissions mitigation challenge and concluded that government intervention in the form of progressive, redistributive carbon taxes and/or cap and trade or cap-and-dividend schemes is the best means of achieving rapid, incentive-driven emissions reduction. Greenhouse emissions are a market externality, which for the psychological and other reasons discussed above, are not priced effectively (if at all) by free markets.

Fifthly, our greenhouse emissions are themselves a symptom of a more fundamental problem to do with our **relentless pursuit of growth**: consumption growth and economic growth, the engine of which is population growth. Statistician and demographer Hans Rosling[xi] has demonstrated that the global population should peak at around 10 billion people by the middle of this century. That's just 35 years to add an extra three billion people. Mind you, in the previous 35 years the earth's population rose by 66% (from 4.3 billion in the late 1970s to 7.1 billion in 2013), so it's not at all unrealistic.

Whereas global food productivity managed to keep pace with the last 35 years of expansion, that was due to the so-called green revolution launched by the plant breeder Norman Borlaug in India, which pushed synthetic fertilisers and other techniques across the globe, while also exploiting vast new tracts of increasingly marginal arable land. Those techniques have created new problems such as leached or salinised soils and agricultural run-off polluting and endangering many river, lake and coastal ecosystems. Not to mention exploited fisheries and significant methane emissions from cows and sheep.

Now that we've used up most of the tricks in the green revolution playbook, we're going to need a new script to feed the next three billion mouths.

No wonder, therefore, that a powerful and insidious denialist movement – funded by organisations and individuals with a vested interest in maintaining the fossil-fuel leadership status quo (and starring some of the very same actors previously involved in the denial of the health risks of tobacco) is actively spreading doubt about the science and fear about the economic impacts of doing something to reduce global emissions. And doing so while also ignoring or downplaying the potentially catastrophic impacts, both economic and environmental, of doing nothing. The extent of these activities is well documented in Erik Conway and Naomi Oreskes' 2010 book Merchants of Doubt.

The denialists' misinformation campaign has been so successful that a recent survey[xii] in the United Kingdom found that despite the almost unequivocal scientific consensus, only one in nine respondents (11%) understood that the science is settled. Another 11% thought that a majority of scientists actually rejected the notion that humans are to blame for climate change and 35% thought scientists were evenly split on the issue. Other surveys[xiii] have found only a small majority (56%) agree with the statement that "climate change is happening and is mostly caused by humans".

With all these factors conspiring against meaningful action to curtail emissions, global attempts to implement binding emissions reduction targets have stalled or failed in recent years. And each year without deep emissions cuts makes the prospect of avoiding significant levels of climate change (and along with it a host of mostly negative impacts) more remote.

Even the landmark deal reached in Paris in December 2015 falls well short of what is required, with the combined national commitments estimated to reduce business as usual greenhouse emissions only sufficient to still lock in at least 2.7 degrees Celsius of global increase (down from four degrees). The agreement won't take effect until 2020 and in any case needs to be ratified by individual countries. And of course countries then need to make good on their pledges, which will require multi-trillion dollar investments and the mothballing of various emissions intensive activities (more on that later).[xiv] Some governments will face significant political pressure to avoid that spend or divert it to other projects.

Delay in implementing a solution is not the smart solution.

To borrow terminology from the game of cricket, the current "required run rate" is around a 6% global reduction in carbon emissions every year to keep average temperature increases within the two degrees Celsius so-called "safe" limit. The current trajectory: between 2012 and 2013 global anthropogenic emissions were estimated to have risen by 2.3%, with a forecast 2014 growth rate of 2.5%.[xv]

In short, climate change is a so-called "wicked problem",[xvi] characterised by "incomplete or contradictory knowledge, the number of people and opinions involved, the large economic burden, and the interconnected nature of these problems with other problems".

However, this book is not about trying to convince you that global warming or climate change is real. It's only going to talk incidentally about limiting your emissions of greenhouse gases or reducing your personal or organisational environmental footprint.

Rather, we're starting with the following assumptions, based on what science and our observations of human behaviour tell us:

1. global warming is occurring and its effects are already being experienced;

2. it has largely been caused by human activities;

3. it's causing a chain reaction of climatic and environmental consequences;

4. global action to limit emissions significantly may not happen in time to prevent irreversible and significant levels of warming; and therefore,

5. we're going to need to adapt to those impacts.

Climate change has many downsides. In time, our society will be irrevocably altered in ways that will cause immense suffering and limit the opportunities of billions of people. Some communities and businesses are already feeling the initial impacts today. We'll address the business impacts in the following chapters.

But there are also plenty of opportunities for organisations prepared to transform themselves to meet the climate challenge.

Our society will need new, sustainably produced products and services to help us:

1. reduce our greenhouse emissions to avoid environmental impact (a process that is generally referred to as mitigation);

2. adapt to the impacts of a changing climate (adaptation);

3. reverse the environmental degradation that we have caused the planet; and

4. engineer a more sustainable, steady-state economy.[4]

Indeed, a raft of reports have been released in the last year or so from regional and global think tanks and supranational organisations including the World Bank[xvii], the UN IPCC 5th Assessment Report, Working Group II – Impacts, Adaptation and Vulnerability[xviii], the Risky Business[xix] think tank (led by notable US Republican Hank Paulson, the former Secretary to the US Treasury during the George W Bush Presidency and Independent Michael Bloomberg, the previous Mayor of New York) and the Global Commission on the Economy and Climate. These reports all point to the clear economic benefits inherent in transitioning to a new way of doing business.

We call it the Adaptive Economy.

This book is aimed at business owners seeking an edge for their organisations in the Adaptive Economy.

In **Part 1** we're going to look at the downside risks of climate change: what it actually means for businesses and how they should go about assessing their risk levels. Then in **Part 2** we'll look at the growing range of opportunities for new products and services that is being created by growing awareness and experience of the impacts of a changing climate and its causes. **Part 3** considers the limitations of many corporate sustainability programs and steps

---

4   There's also a fifth business prospect, which is simply to exploit market opportunities caused by a changing climate, and the environment be damned. One such example is moves by major oil companies to extract oil from under the Arctic ocean in areas that have recently become accessible due to ice melt. It's a sad irony that the improved accessibility is caused by the burning of fossil fuels including oil. It's a perverse form of profiteering but perhaps a harbinger of the wild west opportunism and self interest that lies in store.

to crafting a strategy for your business that will propel it forward into the Adaptive Economy.

A quick primer on climate change science

Without the earth's atmosphere, and in particular the so-called greenhouse gases it contains, the average surface temperature of our planet would be a freezing -18 degrees Centigrade as opposed to the average 14°C we enjoyed during much of the 20th century.[xx] Much of the heat received from the sun would simply radiate back into space.

Much like the glass in a greenhouse, these gases (including Carbon Dioxide, Methane, Nitrous Oxide, water vapour, and also more recently certain gases used in TV screens, and refrigerants/propellants such as CFCs and HFCs) trap heat within the atmosphere and reflect it back towards the surface, warming the earth. Each of these gases occurs in the atmosphere in differing concentrations.

Historically, the relative concentrations of pre-industrial gases mostly remained fairly static, as natural processes (such as photosynthesis by plants, respiration by animals and the exchange of gases between the atmosphere and the oceans) maintained equilibrium levels. Every so often, however, something occurs to disrupt this equilibrium.

Before the start of the industrial era, atmospheric Carbon Dioxide levels have been estimated at around 280 parts per million (ppm). Carbon Dioxide is essential to the process of photosynthesis in plants, but a little goes a long way. Too much causes the earth's temperature to rise, and we have evidence of that derived from ice cores and other long term climate records going back around 800,000 years. What these tell us (combined with other evidence) is that the earth's climate has repeatedly gone through cooler and warmer periods, with the changes immediately preceded by variations in Carbon Dioxide concentrations.

The keeping of accurate records of atmospheric Carbon Dioxide commenced in Hawaii in the late-1950s, and they are now measured at a variety of stations at remote locations around the world. At that time the concentration was about 312ppm. In April 2014 it hit 400ppm for the first time. That's an increase of 28% in under 60 years.

Not only is the atmospheric concentration of Carbon Dioxide now at levels not seen in nearly a million years worth of data, the speed of the change is unprecedented. The growth rate has accelerated from 1ppm per annum in the 1960s to over 2ppm per annum in the 2000s.[xxi]

The concentrations of other greenhouse gases have also been increasing. Each has a different ability to trap heat within the atmosphere over a given time scale, a measure known as global warming potential (GWP).

A kilogram of Carbon Dioxide has a GWP of one and lasts in the atmosphere for centuries, whereas a kilogram of some of the compounds found in your TV persist for up to 50,000 years and are more potent greenhouse gases with a GWP in the thousands. Methane, on the other hand, is a potent but fairly short-lived atmospheric gas with a GWP of 72 over 20 years, but this drops away over longer time scales.[xxii] Atmospheric water vapour concentrations depend on temperature, with more evaporation from oceans, lakes and soils occurring as temperatures increase – therefore compounding the greenhouse effect.

Aggregate weather records indicate that global average surface temperatures have increased by around one degree Celsius since the current warming trend began about a century ago. Global average temperature records were broken in 2014 and again in 2015. The warming effect is not felt evenly and is particularly concentrated in the Arctic and northern Eurasia.

Global climate change events in the past, such as the ice ages, are thought to have been triggered by various natural phenomena including volcanic eruptions (which spray sulfur dioxide and other chemicals high into the atmosphere and therefore tend to have a cooling effect on global temperatures); solar activity such as sun-spots (which change the level of heat reaching earth); eccentricities in earth's orbit around the sun (changing the average distance to the earth's heat source); and normal climate variability (such as the El Niño / La Niña cycle in the Pacific Ocean).

The impacts of these changes can change rates of photosynthesis and other processes that affect the concentrations of greenhouse gases.

BUT – the big difference this time around is that scientists have ruled out natural triggers. So what's causing the change?

Since the start of industrial times in the late 18th century, humans have extracted and burnt for energy hundreds of billion tonnes of fossil fuels (coal, oil and gas). Burning a kilogram of coal produces about 2.4kg of Carbon Dioxide (since there are two Oxygen atoms added to each Carbon atom to make the molecule, each of which has a greater weight than the Carbon itself). It's fairly similar for oil and gas.[xxiii] Meanwhile we've also released carbon trapped in trees and soils through land clearing and deforestation.

In the wake of the UN-convened Rio Earth Summit in 1992, governments around the world have been preparing national inventories of greenhouse gas emissions related to human activities (known as anthropogenic emissions) in accordance with the UN Framework Convention on Climate Change (UN FCCC). In 2011 the global estimated anthropogenic Carbon Dioxide emissions were in the order of 34 billion tonnes.[xxiv]

A simple calculation helps make the point.[5] The earth's atmosphere is estimated to weigh about five trillion (million million) tonnes. This means that each 2 parts per million increase in Carbon Dioxide concentration is equivalent to about 10 billion tonnes – accounting for about half of the estimated human emissions. A lot of the extra greenhouse gases being produced by humans are absorbed by the oceans and mix with water to become carbonic acid, increasing acidity levels.[xxv] Some is absorbed by trees through the process of photosynthesis; much of the rest is being soaked up in soils.[6]

It's this human-induced increase in greenhouse gases that is believed to be the principal cause of the observed global warming trend. Based on a variety of data sources, the global average temperature in the first decade of the 21st century is estimated to be warmer that at any time in the last 2,000 years, including the so called Medieval Warm Period between the 10th and 12th centuries.[xxvi] And it's likely to get a lot hotter.

In the next chapter we will look more at the impacts of this change.

---

5   This calculation is provided for illustrative purposes only and does not reflect all the factors at work in global atmospheric cycles. Note that the oxygen atoms in a carbon dioxide molecule are already in the atmosphere at the point they combine with fossil fuel carbon through the combustion process.

6   It's worth noting though, that in most of the places emissions are highest there are fewer and fewer trees or other vegetation – or even exposed soil – to absorb the CO2 due to land clearing and urban development.

PART 1
RISK

*"When our leaders accept
the status quo, we run
the risk of disaster."*

Max Bazerman

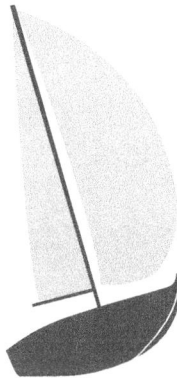

Chapter 1
The Climate is
Changing – So What?

The weather dictates many aspects of our lives: for example, what we wear; whether we go out or stay in; whether our commute will be longer or shorter; the cost of our insurance; what we eat (or how much it costs); and our housing. Actually, humans are pretty adaptable and can be found living in all manner of climates, from the sweltering tropics to the Arctic circle. You'll find people living in different regions where average temperatures are tens of degrees apart, from the tropics to far northern Canada, for example. Even in the same place, temperature extremes between summer highs and winter lows can be 60 degrees Celsius apart or more.

When I migrated from my native New Zealand to Australia in the late 1990s, I went from a yearly mean temperature of around 13 degrees Celsius to around 18 degrees. It felt hot at first, but within about a year I had acclimatised and after that, whenever I went back to New Zealand I took extra layers of clothing, or felt like I was freezing. In the mid-latitudes (south or north of the tropics), the average temperature changes about 5 degrees C for every 10 degrees of latitude (about 1,100 kilometres of North/South distance).

The UN IPCC's most dire prediction of the change in global mean temperatures by the end of the twenty first century is four to five degrees: about the same as the change I experienced and adapted to. So what's all the fuss about?

Accurate records charting surface temperatures over the majority of the earth began around 100 years ago. Based on World Meteorological Organisation (WMO) data, the global average air temperature during that period was around 14 degrees.[xxvii] However, scientists have a number of other sophisticated ways of estimating what the average temperatures and carbon dioxide concentrations have been over periods of tens of thousands of years or longer, ranging from tree ring data (effective for the last several hundred years), ice core samples (some of which provide evidence dating back

800,000 years) and additional evidence from the geological remains of glacial advances and retreats.

One of the things those methods tell us is that the difference in global average temperatures between the last major Ice Age (about 20,000 years ago) and current times is about five degrees.[xxviii] That difference was enough to lower global sea levels by about 120 metres. North America and Northern Europe were permanently covered in ice up to several kilometres thick, down to the latitude of the northern United States.

That five degree change from the previous temperate climate to Ice Age is estimated to have taken place over millenia. We're now talking about a potential change of four to five degrees over one century.

Global changes in average temperature, even apparently small ones, represent massive shifts in the amount of energy being stored in the atmosphere and oceans. That extra energy causes new weather. Extreme weather. Like superstorms Hurricane Sandy (New York, 2012) and Typhoon Haiyan (also known as Yolanda, which devastated the Philippines in 2013).

According to the IPCC, climate change is expected to concentrate the weather into more violent storms, more heat waves, harsher prolonged droughts, changing rainfall patterns, and – perhaps paradoxically – extreme cold snaps such as the so-called polar vortex seen in parts of North America during the 2014 winter.

Explaining these phenomena requires a detailed understanding of the global weather system, which is driven by interactions between the temperature of the air, oceans and land masses, resultant patterns of evaporation, ocean currents and the coriolis effect of earth's rotation on the atmosphere amongst other factors.[xxix] The polar vortex is thought to have been caused by a weakening of the jet stream air flow over North America, caused by warming in the Arctic interacting with tropical air streams and allowing an intense low pressure system to stall over central eastern North America.

Here's why it matters

Extreme weather has downstream impacts such as more intense bush fires, landslips and soil erosion, desertification, crop losses, storm surges, flooding and property damage. The decline of alpine snow packs and glaciers is threatening the water supplies of billions of people. Over the next 30-70 years, we may have to abandon the idea of one-in-a-hundred year events as they become more like disastrous annual occurrences.

That's on land. In the oceans, some of the extra greenhouse gases are dissolving, creating carbonic acid and increasing the acidity of the water. This is directly affecting creatures near the bottom of the food chain such as corals and crustaceans, whose protective shells are dissolving. In turn acidification reduces oxygen levels in sea water, potentially making large tracts of the oceans barren.

Increasing water temperature near the surface is already affecting the oceans' currents and nutrient conveyors. These changes will affect marine life and weather patterns in ways we still don't fully understand. One mooted change is the potential decline of the North Atlantic Drift, which transports warm waters from the Gulf Stream past the United Kingdom and Northern Europe, bringing with it a much more temperate climate to that part of the world than would otherwise be the case.[xxx]

And then there's sea level rise. If cooling of five degrees lowered sea levels by 120 metres, warming could lead to significant rising through melting land ice and, initially, thermal expansion of the oceans. The rising trend is already observable, with global levels up around 20cm over the last century, and the rate of rise accelerating.

The good news is that the IPCC's current worst-case prediction for sea level rise during this century is a mere 1.2m. However, that's still enough to seriously impact the coastal infrastructure of many of the world's great cities, particularly when combined with storm surges from extreme weather.

Should, for example, all the ice on Greenland melt, it would add about seven metres (although that would play out over a much longer time horizon, as would the collapse of the Antarctic ice sheets). Sea level rise will be more pronounced in some areas given the effects of currents, tides and the contours of the sea bed. And even if we only get the indicated level this century, we'll probably be looking at additional sea level rise for many centuries to come.

Figure 1 illustrates the way we're diverting from our known climate norms into unknown territory.

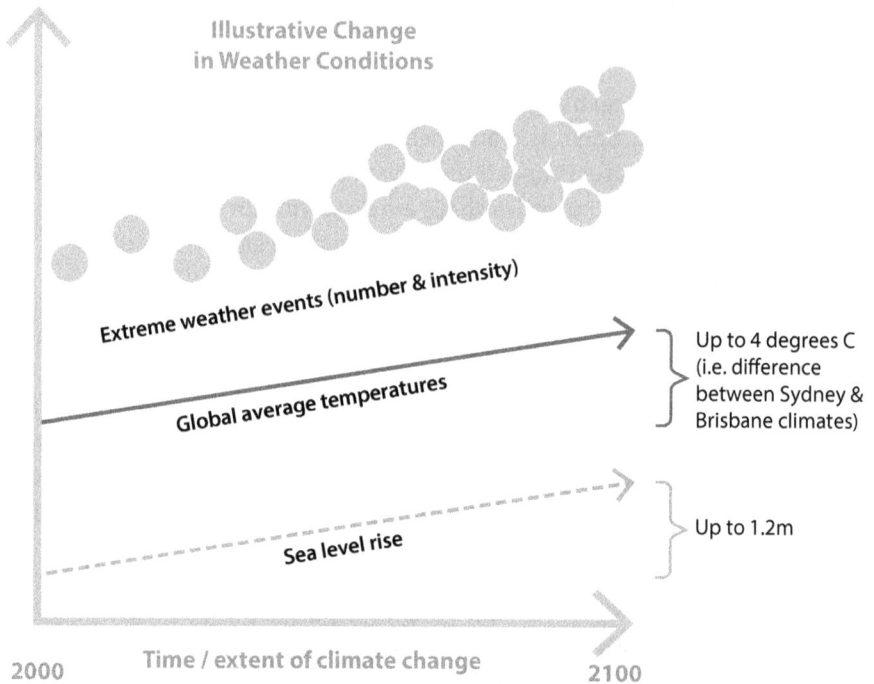

Illustrative Change in Weather Conditions

Extreme weather events (number & intensity)

Global average temperatures

Up to 4 degrees C (i.e. difference between Sydney & Brisbane climates)

Sea level rise

Up to 1.2m

2000

Time / extent of climate change

2100

Figure 1 – Impacts of a changing climate

In mountainous and polar areas, another threat is beginning to emerge: increased seismic and volcanic activity as the land decompresses due to the reduced weight of melting ice. For example, measurements have indicated that the island of Iceland is currently rising at the rate of 3.5cm per year.[xxxi] Volcanic activity on the island has increased in recent years – leading to several significant shutdowns of European commercial air space – and it is thought there may be a link between the two phenomena.

A rise in global average temperatures changes local temperature ranges, but by varying amounts depending on factors such as prevailing winds (which might also change), ocean currents and interactions between land and water masses. Some areas will see average temperatures rise by significantly more than the global average; some by less; and some areas may actually see a decline in local averages.

This is a reason why Climate Change is a more appropriate moniker for the effects, while Global Warming is used to describe the overall warming trend. This temperature variation (combined with changing wind and rainfall patterns plus other extreme weather) will affect the production of food crops and threaten fragile ecosystems. Millions of plant and animal species could become extinct.

In areas where temperatures rise, the likelihood of disease rises through the spread of infection carrying mosquitos and other disease vectors. Health systems may also be strained by other challenges including increased incidence of heat stroke and dehydration, illnesses from contaminated water supplies or flooded sewage systems following storm damage, malnutrition following crop failures, and injuries associated with super storms or bush fires.

A changing climate challenges infrastructure including cities; transport systems such as ports and low lying coastal airports and roads; telecommunications and energy networks exposed to storm damage; water supplies; agricultural irrigation systems; and coastal property. Labour productivity may suffer, particularly for outdoor work. And energy demand will increase as people struggle to stay cool.

It's already impacting bottom lines

We're already seeing a sharply growing damage bill from extreme weather, with the global number of extreme weather events *doubling* in the last 30 years as shown in Figure 2.[7] Most of the other effects of climate change will come more gradually.

The analogy of a frog in a pot of water on the stove[8] has been used by Al Gore and others to describe how our avarice, arrogance and apathy (as termed in the Pulitzer Prize winning Inside Climate News[xxxiii]) may prevent meaningful action – either towards mitigation or adaptation – until it's too late.

---

7   Normalised from global reinsurer Munich Re's data by prominent climate change blogger Grant Foster.

8   This apocryphal analogy refers to idea frogs are unable to sense slow increases in their surrounding temperatures, so if one is put in a pot of water and the water slowly brought to the boil, a frog will not be aware of the need to jump out until it is too late to save itself from being a cooked frog. While it's an oft-used tale, it is not scientifically true (unlike climate change) as James Fallon, writing in The Atlantic points out.[xxxii]

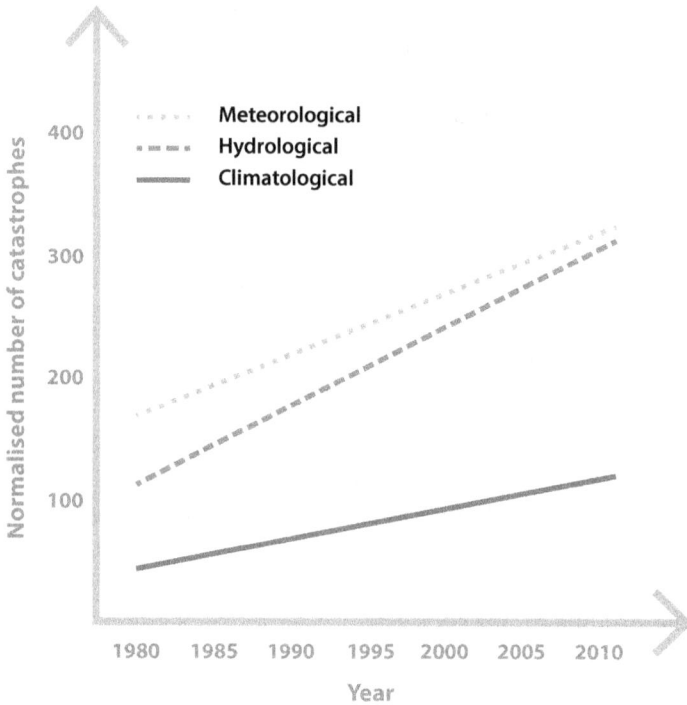

Figure 2 – Normalised global extreme weather catastrophes[xxxiv]

Now let's look at this from a business perspective. Already, your organisation is exposed to potential impacts from severe weather. Depending on where they're located, your shops, offices, warehouses, factories, farms, mines and/or vehicles may be at risk of damage from flooding, storms, bush fire and other natural disasters. Such damage can be costly to repair, and may interrupt your ability to do business. So you have insurance policies in place, possibly including business interruption cover as a contingency. You may also have disaster recovery plans and emergency arrangements.

But will these arrangements be sufficient in light of the impacts of climate change? And will insurance remain affordable or effective given the spiraling premium costs seen in the last decade and the expectation of more frequent and severe extreme weather events in the years to come?

It comes down to sound risk assessment

For business, climate change should be considered in terms of risk, which is a combination of the probability of an occurrence in a given time horizon and the impact (monetary or otherwise) if it occurs. What insurers are already experiencing is that the probability is increasing: extreme weather event are occurring more frequently. And the impacts are increasing as the severity or intensity of extreme weather grows. Each particular potential threat or hazard associated with a changing climate will have a different combination of probability and impact – and therefore risk – for each organisation.

The potential business impacts of a risk can be numerous and include:

- Damage to property, plant and equipment, leading to repair costs and operational interruptions.

- Interruption to the company's upstream supply chain, if its suppliers are affected by a disaster.

- Loss of revenue, for example due to lost sales if a business cannot operate.

- Loss of revenue, but this time if customers are adversely impacted by an event and/or demand for a company's products or services dries up (temporarily or permanently).

- Damage to the company's reputation if it is unable to service its customers. This also flows through to loss of revenue.

- Regulatory or legal consequences of being unable to operate or lacking the cash-flow to meet working capital requirements.

- Increased costs arising from the clean up or recovery process, which may not be fully covered by insurance policies.

This description of impacts is oriented towards events that occur suddenly. But bear in mind some risks are more insidious and can be harder to spot: for example, a declining sales trend played out over 20 or 30 years due to a product becoming increasingly less attractive due to rising environmental concerns amongst consumers: again, the frog in the pot analogy applies.

Risks can be treated in several ways as highlighted in the risk matrix table in Figure 3:[9]

9   Adapted from the ISO 31000 Risk Management Standard.

Probability of occurance (in a given time frame)	Impact of occurence				
	Insignificant	Minor	Moderate	Major	Catastrophic
Almost Certain					
Likely					
Moderate					
Unlikely					
Rare					

Minor Risk	**Moderate Risk**	**Significant Risk**	**Severe Risk**
Accept; factor into control measures	Implement control measures	Corrective action needed	Discontinue activity immediately/ urgent corrective action required

Figure 3 – A typical risk matrix

Low probability and lower impact risks can often be accepted and dealt with using normal operational controls. In the case of lower probability but higher impact risks some of the financial impacts can often be transferred cost effectively using insurance. Higher probability risks should be treated in order to reduce the probability of occurrence, starting with those risks with the highest potential impacts. Low probability but high impact risks can typically be dealt with using contingency plans and emergency preparedness measures.

With climate change, three things happen to the risk matrix as highlighted in Figure 4:

1. A range of existing hazards, such as extreme weather, increase in probability and impact as time passes, moving towards the top right of the matrix. In other words it acts as a threat multiplier.

2. New phenomena, such as sea level rise or water shortages, may become high probability – if not certain – events, albeit in a longer time horizon. The extent of their impact depends on the type of business, its locations and markets served.

3. As probability and impact levels increase, insurance as a risk transfer option becomes increasingly unaffordable and ineffective. More emphasis must be placed on risk mitigation and contingency measures.

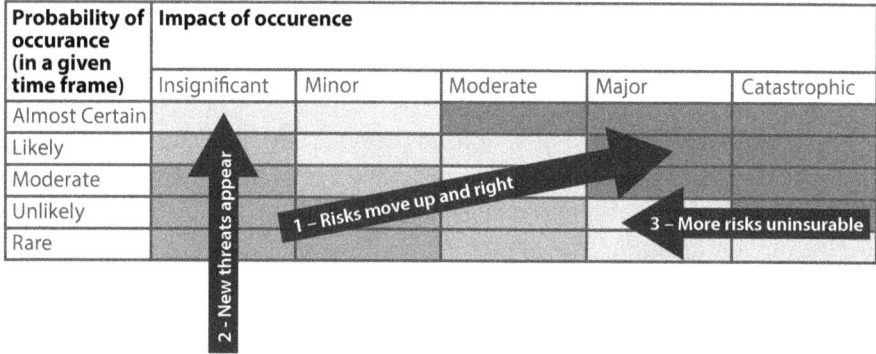

Probability of occurance (in a given time frame)	Impact of occurence				
	Insignificant	Minor	Moderate	Major	Catastrophic
Almost Certain					
Likely					
Moderate					
Unlikely					
Rare					

1 – Risks move up and right

2 - New threats appear

3 – More risks uninsurable

Figure 4 – How climate change impacts the risk matrix

Let's think about what factors might affect an organisation's exposure to climate change impacts.

First of all it's important to get past the extreme weather impacts and look more deeply at what's likely to happen. It's one thing to consider your organisation's operations, or your suppliers or customers being impacted by super storms or other localised events. But what may have more impact on your business in the short to medium term is a change to regulatory arrangements affecting input prices (such as a carbon pricing mechanism). It doesn't matter if you're a power station or a corner store: a carbon price may cause the cost of many of your inputs to rise.

The bottom line is, the less fossil fuel-dependent (or otherwise emissions intensive) your energy and other key inputs are, the more competitive your business will be relative to that of other players in your industry.

If you do happen to be a major producer or consumer of fossil fuels, or a major emitter of greenhouse gases through other means (such as land clearing, cement production or other industrial processes), then get set for reputational damage and subsequent loss of market share and/or shareholder value. This is coming from two main directions:

- A global "divestment" movement targeting superannuation and endowment funds and banks is gaining pace. Its objective is to convince institutional investors of the folly of holding stocks in "fossil fuel-exposed" industries including coal, oil and gas extractors and distributors on the grounds that the value of such investments is likely to decline, perhaps sharply when it becomes clear that a lot of their assets (coal, oil and gas deposits and reserves) cannot be extracted, sold or burnt, therefore becoming "stranded assets".[xxxv] This may also happen if governments legislate deep emissions reduction targets.

- A growing movement of green groups actively targeting corporates involved in perpetuating the extraction and use of fossil fuels (or other environmentally harmful activities). These organisations are typically moving more rapidly than governments. They are building a groundswell of opposition, encouraging boycotts and generally garnering negative publicity about the companies they attack.

The divestment movement originated from a range of sources. On the one hand are organisations led by environmentalists, such as Bill McKibben's 350. org. What's more interesting are the organisations led by the "elder states-people" of politics and business.

In Australia one such manifestation is the Asset Owners' Disclosure Project (AODP), fronted by John Hewson, the former leader of the right wing Australian Liberal Party and one of the original Macquarie Group investment banking team.

The AODP encourages asset owners in the form of superannuation and endowment funds around the world to disclose their exposure to fossil fuel intensive investments through a questionnaire process. It then names and shames organsations, and this has reportedly led to a number of significant divestment announcements by various funds. The combination of political and/or business influence appears to provide boardroom credibility that goes beyond what a group of well meaning activists can muster.

Meanwhile, there are risks awaiting a range of relatively benign industries whose businesses depend on conditions that may be detrimentally impacted by climate change. This includes companies that form part of the supply chains of core fossil-fuel firms: the likes of oil and gas pipeline builders; mining engineers; manufacturers of coal loading equipment and so on.

Even much loved companies like toy-maker Lego have been singled out, in that case due to their implicit support of oil major Royal Dutch Shell through the sale of co-branded product in Shell's stores. Greenpeace was behind a 2014 campaign that included a very effective viral video and online petition signed by hundreds of thousands of people world-wide.

The campaign's objective was to draw attention to Shell's plans to extract oil from Arctic areas that have recently been made accessible due to warming caused by anthropogenic climate change. Of course the campaign also chides Lego for its association with Shell (which has reportedly been profitable for both firms, boosting sales at Shell petrol stations) and may have adversely impacted the purity of its branding. After several months' contemplation Lego announced in October 2014 that it would not renew its lucrative contract with Shell.

On the other hand, what about alpine sports or coral coast tourism? Climate change is already threatening ski resorts around the globe, with milder winters leading to ever-shorter seasons with less snow cover. Many coral reefs are stressed from a combination of warming ocean waters, growing acidity from dissolved carbon dioxide (making it harder for the corals to form hard calcium-based structures), pollution from agricultural runoff and other sources and a range of other issues.

Tourism operators and their suppliers whose livelihoods depend on good snow or a healthy reef may be decimated within a few short decades as their draw card assets are destroyed by climate change. In Australia, the ski industry is worth about A$1.8 billion[xxxvi] per annum while the Great Barrier Reef is estimated to contribute over A$6 billion annually to the local economy.[xxxvii] The loss of the Reef would further devastate the state of Queensland, which has an economy that is also heavily dependent on coal, gas and oil mining. Tourism is far more labour intensive than mining, with Australia's skiing and coral coast assets estimated to provide employment to over 80,000 people.

Food producers face an uncertain future. Changing patterns of rainfall and drought, coupled with destructive storms and gradually increasing temperatures will make crop yields and prices more volatile. The imposition of carbon taxes or trading schemes may increase costs for farmers and food producers, affecting, for example, the use of vehicles for harvesting and transporting crops and the cost of pumping irrigation water. When methane emissions from livestock are also taken into account, meat prices will rise further.

Then there are companies such as the airlines, whose costs are increasing due to climate change. Not necessarily, as one might expect, due to the imposition of a carbon pricing mechanism increasing the cost of their fuel, but actually because the changing climate is adversely affecting wind patterns, meaning more fuel is consumed.[xxxvii]

How about coastal communities? As storm surges increase and sea level rise becomes more apparent, councils will be forced to spend more on sea walls, drainage, beach replenishment and other defenses, necessitating potentially significant rate rises. Meanwhile, some local authorities are already floating the idea of developmental restrictions in low lying coastal areas, which could have a devastating impact on property values for owners and investors.

Identifying the weakest links in your supply chain

In today's world of globalised commerce, supply chain risks are becoming ever more diverse and important to manage. In response to consumer demand following campaigns about the exploitation of child labour, deplorable pay or working conditions, use of genetically modified crops or other issues, we've seen organisations begin to actively trace materials as they move through the production process.

Thus, I can use the Internet to find out from which New Zealand high country farm the Merino wool in my winter cycling vest was sourced, simply by entering the code on the label, and learn about the environment the contributing sheep were raised in. On my ride I can enjoy my chocolate bar safe in the knowledge that the cacao beans it was made from can be traced back to a farm on the other side of the world where the workers are appropriately paid and looked after.

At a business-to-business level, though, how do I find out about the risks of disruption to my supply chain caused by climate change? Where do the materials in my products originate? How well prepared are the original and intermediate suppliers to deal with the effects? What are my logistics exposures given the land, sea and/or air shipping routes involved? And since extreme weather events often cause regional or national-level impacts and require a government-led response, what is the capacity of the countries and jurisdictions involved to avoid adverse impacts and minimise damage when superstorms, droughts and other supply chain-affecting events hit?

The answers are often far from clear, but a range of new tools are being developed to assist supply chain and logistics managers. One example at a country level is Notre Dame University's Global Adaptation Index (ND-GAIN),[xxxix] which combines measures of each nation's vulnerability to the impacts of a changing climate with an estimate of its capacity to adapt given its financial, legal and other resources and institutions.

At a more granular level, our research has led to the development of the Adaptive Capability Maturity Model (Adaptive CMM), which provides a rating for an individual organisation highlighting its progress towards sustainability and climate-change readiness based on the assessment of several hundred factors.

Organisations procuring goods and services from other companies can use the Adaptive CMM to assess the health of their supply-chain providers. We'll return to the methodology and findings in a later chapter.

Chapter 2
A New Risk Model

Here's another way of looking at climate change risks, using two key dimensions of the organisation's strategic impact; and its operational resilience.

Strategic impact is assessed along a scale between negative, neutral and positive depending on the size of the organisation's direct and/or indirect environmental impact – its greenhouse emissions, water use, waste production, environmental degradation and other pollution; up and down its supply chain. At the positive end of the continuum, an organisation is, on balance, environmentally beneficial rather than harmful. Neutral and negatively positioned organisations may face strategic pressures such as:

- Increased costs (either incurred directly or passed on by suppliers) due to the imposition of carbon prices.

- Regulation affecting the organisation's license to operate.

- Reputation damage due to perceptions of the organisation's environmental stance.

- Increasing costs of capital if investors become wary of potential stranded assets.

- Declining market for its products or services, particularly if alternatives with more positive strategic impact are available. In some cases alternatives could become more attractive to customers because they offer lower operating emissions (and therefore relatively lower running costs).

- A company's association with or reliance on organisations with a negative strategic impact will affect that firm's positioning on the scale, since this may indicate that the market for its services will in turn decline.

Operational resilience uses a scale between exposed and resilient to assess how the organisation will fare as the various effects of climate change become more intense. A company's position along this dimension is affected by factors such as:

- The extent to which its success depends on the local climate remaining static. Alpine sports, coral coast tourism, seafood and agriculture are particularly climate sensitive.
- Its specific operating locations, including those of its supply chain providers and the downstream customers and end users of its products / services.
- How exposed its assets (property and plant) are to extreme weather, warming, changing rainfall patterns and other climate change impacts. A business in the agricultural sector would generally be more climate sensitive than an office-based services company.
- How long term and significant its capital investments are (organisations whose business model depends on capital intensive, illiquid, long term assets exploited over 30+ years are significantly more exposed to the effects of climate change as its impacts become more apparent).

Refined to the two dimensions of impact and resilience, a particular company's current climate change risk profile can be plotted on a matrix as depicted in Figure 5.

A company's position on this matrix is organization-specific and reflects a point in time. Different firms within the same industry may occupy relatively divergent positions on the matrix depending on their unique circumstances. An organisation can move along one or both dimensions over time depending on the decisions it makes.

Figure 6 shows how different industries fare on this scale – bearing in mind that different companies in the same industry can have different outcomes depending on their specific situation.

The matrix shows that organisations that fall into the lower left quadrant face an uncertain future unless they embark on a radical transformation program. In general all businesses should be seeking to move towards the top right quadrant. For businesses, this involves:

- sun-setting emissions intensive and other environmentally harmful activities;

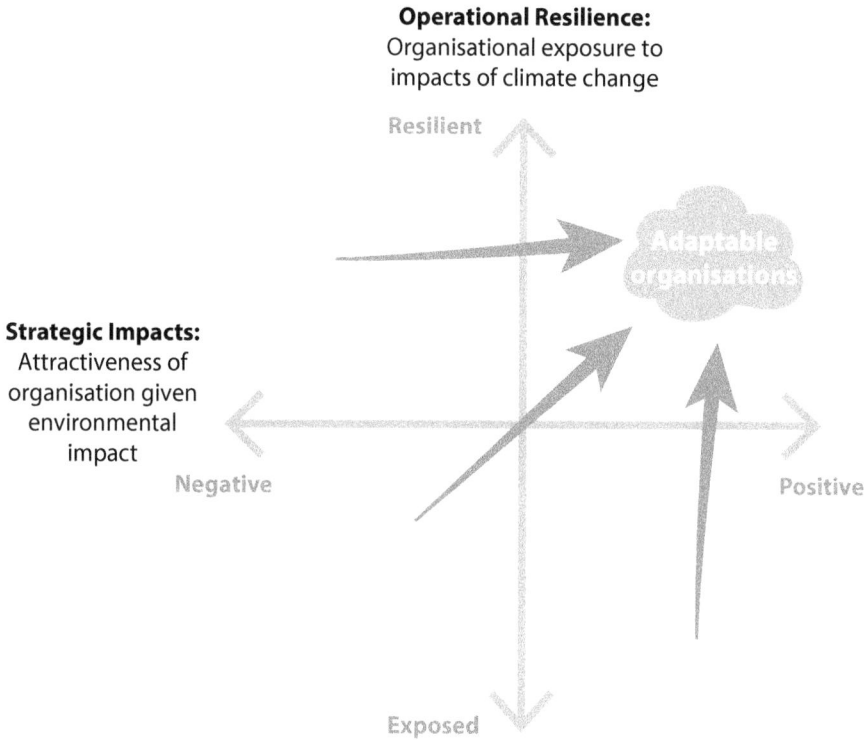

Operational Resilience:
Organisational exposure to
impacts of climate change

Resilient

Adaptable organisations

Strategic Impacts:
Attractiveness of
organisation given
environmental
impact

Negative

Positive

Exposed

Figure 5 – Key dimensions of organisational climate risk

- reviewing and re-engineering supply chains, product and service designs, processes and so on to make them as environmentally sustainable as possible (mitigation);

- reducing risk by putting measures in place to avoid (i.e. reduce the probability) and soften the impact of emerging climate risks; and/or

- exiting or changing businesses where success will be adversely affected by changes in climate.

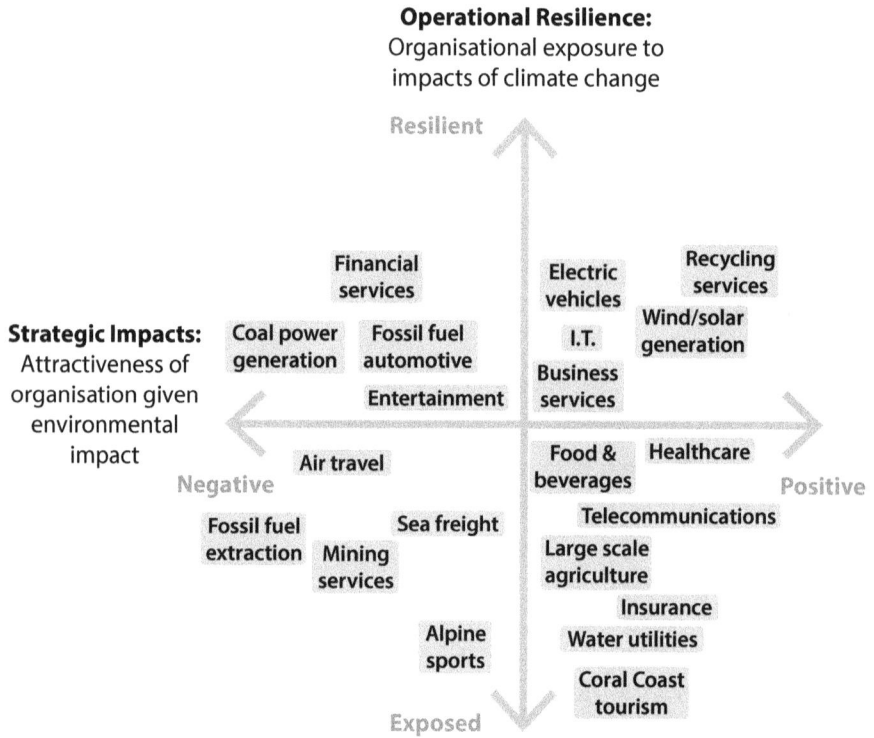

Operational Resilience:
Organisational exposure to
impacts of climate change

Resilient

Strategic Impacts:
Attractiveness of
organisation given
environmental
impact

Negative

Positive

Exposed

Financial services

Electric vehicles

Recycling services

Coal power generation

Fossil fuel automotive

I.T.

Wind/solar generation

Entertainment

Business services

Air travel

Food & beverages

Healthcare

Fossil fuel extraction

Sea freight

Telecommunications

Mining services

Large scale agriculture

Insurance

Alpine sports

Water utilities

Coral Coast tourism

Figure 6 – Indicative industry positioning

Another way of classifying firms based on their climate and footprint exposures uses the following eight descriptors:

1. **Dirty direct** – the organisation is a major GHG emitter and/or polluter and/or contributes to large scale environmental degradation.

2. **Dirty supply chain** – the organisation uses products sourced from high GHG-emitting, polluting and/or environmental degrading sources.

3. **Dirty product** – the major products produced by the organisation are GHG emissions intensive in use, and/or contribute to other forms of pollution or environmental degradation.

4. **Dirty financier** – the organisation finances businesses or projects that are GHG emissions intensive and/or contribute to other forms of pollution or environmental degradation.

5. **Neutral exposed** – the organisation's products or services are not particularly "dirty" (environmentally harmful) but the industry is exposed to medium term climate change or environmental impacts.

6. **Neutral safe** – the organisation is not particularly "dirty" and the industry is not particularly exposed to climate change or environmental impacts.

7. **Clean perception** – the organisation's products or services are generally perceived to do more environmental good than harm.

8. **Clean genuine** – a lifecycle assessment can validate claims that the organisation, its supply chain and the lifetime use of its products and services do more environmental good than harm.

Climate sensitive business risk

Turning back to the examples of alpine sports and coral coast tourism as highly climate sensitive businesses – if you own assets in or are dependent on these industries, you have two choices: sell early while valuations are robust, or wait.

What might happen for those who wait? This will depend on a variety of factors including the speed of decline of the underlying tourism asset (i.e. the decline in the amount of snow and the health of the reef ecosystem); what adaptation measures are taken; and, to a lesser extent, how the situation is publicised.

For example, in 2012 an Australian government publication reported that during the previous 60 years in the Snowy Mountains alpine area, home to Australia's modest ski industry, there had been "a 30% decline in snow amounts" and a temperature change equivalent to 100m of altitude. It reported predictions that by 2050, the amount of snow cover remaining on the ground for more than two months could shrink to as little as 4% of current levels.[xl] One can't help but wonder at what point they will cease to be nicknamed 'the Snowies'.

Clearly skiing and snowboarding in Australia are unsustainable in the relatively short term. For an owner of alpine sports businesses such as ski fields, ski and board hire/sales, chair lift maintenance and so on, every poor season brings them closer to financial ruin.

Interestingly, there may be an upward spike in visitor numbers as consumers attempt to enjoy their winter sports while they still can. On the other hand, shorter seasons, bigger crowds and increasingly marginal snow cover and quality will, in time, reverse that trend. Fields in nearby New Zealand may capture a greater share of the Australian market, benefitting from their higher elevations.

In the short term, investors in the artificial snow making industry should do well as ski fields supplement natural snow. However, snow making machines work best at low temperatures (and low humidity) and will cease being effective as temperatures continue to rise. And of course, skiers will be less interested in paying to use slushy, fast melting snow. Snow making machines are also energy and water intensive and therefore may become increasingly expensive to operate – another nail in the coffin as cash-flow becomes tighter for ski field operators.

For purveyors of alpine accommodation, however, the future may be brighter. Around the globe, there are examples of alpine sports areas re-inventing themselves as summer-time destinations. In the North Eastern United States, for example, snow mobile trails are being widened and strengthened to make them suitable for use by four-wheel-drive RVs.[xli]

Summer programs in alpine regions emphasise the scenic and adventure opportunities of their locations, with hiking, mountain-biking, rock climbing and wild-flower viewing becoming popular alternate uses. Such attractions require places to stay and eat, and things to do in the evenings, potentially benefitting existing businesses that support ski fields.

Financial risks

Even services businesses whose supply chains don't extend much beyond computers and office supplies aren't necessarily immune. Take the banking industry, for example.

A bank's assets are its loan portfolios, including mortgages that are secured against property. Many loans are not paid off for up to 30 years, during which time the bank holds the title deeds as security. Hundreds of billions of dollars worth of mortgaged property is in low lying coastal zones, which are already vulnerable to storm surges that will be probably exacerbated by the increasing intensity of extreme weather and, over time, by accelerating sea level rise.

Home owners in exposed areas (such as where there is proven recurrence of flooding or storm surge damage) will be faced with collapsing values for their properties and may be incentivised (or forced) to foreclose on their mortgages, particularly if local government authorities impose bans on development in demonstrably risk-exposed areas – which would further accelerate devaluation. This situation will be further compounded by action by the insurance industry to make coverage for vulnerable property unaffordable or unavailable.

It takes nearly two thirds of the loan term for the bank to recover half of the principal – a particular problem for highly geared properties (high debt to equity ratio) during a period of declining values. Accordingly, banks should be reviewing their loan books and considering measures to insulate their risks.

That covers the resilience dimension of the risk matrix as far as a typical bank goes. Of course they also need to look at their own operational resilience – where are their major locations and what telecommunications and other infrastructure do they rely on that is vulnerable to extreme weather risks?

The other dimension is the strategic impact based on their environmental footprint sensitivity. Being a services-based organisation, a bank's operational footprint is relatively small, consisting mainly of the emissions associated with electricity consumed at their branches, offices and data centres; corporate travel and vehicle fleets; and consumption of paper, computer equipment and so on. So at one level a bank is relatively emissions neutral compared to, say, a manufacturing firm of equivalent scale.

However, the divestment movement mentioned earlier has identified the value of loans made to fossil fuel extraction businesses and targeted banks with the largest coal, oil and gas portfolios, urging the financial institutions' other customers to move their business to alternate providers that do not lend to that industry.

For affected banks that represents both reputational pressure and potential loss of market share. Meanwhile, banks that have lent to fossil-fuel firms on the basis of multi-decadal revenue projections may face a significant bad debt problem due to the stranded assets issue. If government regulation makes coal deposits (and in time oil and gas reserves) "unburnable", such firms' revenue sources will dry up and, in turn, so might their loan repayments.

In reality it is likely that such sanctions would be introduced over a prolonged period of time, which is likely to cushion the financial impacts that might be felt by lenders. However, the business case for lending to new mining projects should be scrutinised intensely.

- Long term capital intensive industries
- Fossil fuel extractors (coal, oil, gas)
- Suppliers to fossil fuel extractors (e.g. oil/gas pipeline layers, mining equipment suppliers)
- Large scale fossil fuel consumers (transport, aluminium, steel)
- Large scale agriculture / food production
- Marine food production
- Logistics / transportation
- Airlines, airports & ports
- Local government
- Organisations with sensitive coastal exposed property / infrastructure
- Banking & insurance
- Specialist tourism (e.g. alpine / coral / islands / beaches)
- Utilities

Table 1 – Sectors at high risk from climate change

The point of this chapter has been to highlight a range of emerging or intensifying business risks that will typify the Adaptive Economy. The risk assessment process is particular to each organisation, depending on their activities, products/services, operating locations, markets served, supply chains, existing risk management processes and other factors.

Depending on what the process reveals, organisations may need to rethink their business strategies and adopt a combination of mitigation and adaptation approaches to improve their footprint sensitivity and climate sensitivity, both in terms of their own operations and also up and down their supply chains. Table 1 highlights a range of at risk sectors.

Classifying impacts

Before we leave the topic of risk, Figure 7 presents another, different matrix, which may be useful in categorising impacts arising from a changing climate. In this case the vertical axis considers whether risks accruing to a particular organisation impact it at a direct, local level or a more regional level or market-wide level. The horizontal axis considers whether risks are of a physical nature (i.e. the direct impacts of climate change such as extreme weather) or whether they impact more on the organisation's reputation or its long term viability.

In the bottom left hand corner (Quadrant 1) we see risks such as localised severe storms directly damaging or impairing the organisation's property and plant. In the top left (Quadrant 2) are regional-scale disasters, which may impair an organisation's labour force (if staff are unable or unwilling to get to work), disrupt utilities and supply chains or otherwise prevent it from servicing its customers, regardless of whether its plant and equipment is directly damaged.

For many businesses, if customers can't get what they want, they switch suppliers, quite quickly in some cases. For example, in the 1980s, the port in Kobe, Japan, was one of the busiest in the world and Japan's principal port. After the Great Hanshin earthquake in 1995, port operations were severely disrupted and many of its customers made alternate arrangements to continue to ship goods through other ports. When Kobe's port reopened, some customers returned their business, but others found their new arrangements satisfactory and continued with them. 20 years later, Kobe's port is only the fourth busiest in Japan and has slipped well down the global rankings.[xlii]

On the flip side, a Quadrant 2 impact could also apply if an organisation's customer-base is impacted in such a way that their demand for its products and services wanes. For smaller businesses serving local markets on a reasonably tight cash-flow this can be a serious. Following major flooding, for example, many communities may find that spending on safety, clean up and rebuilding takes precedence over discretionary or luxury goods.

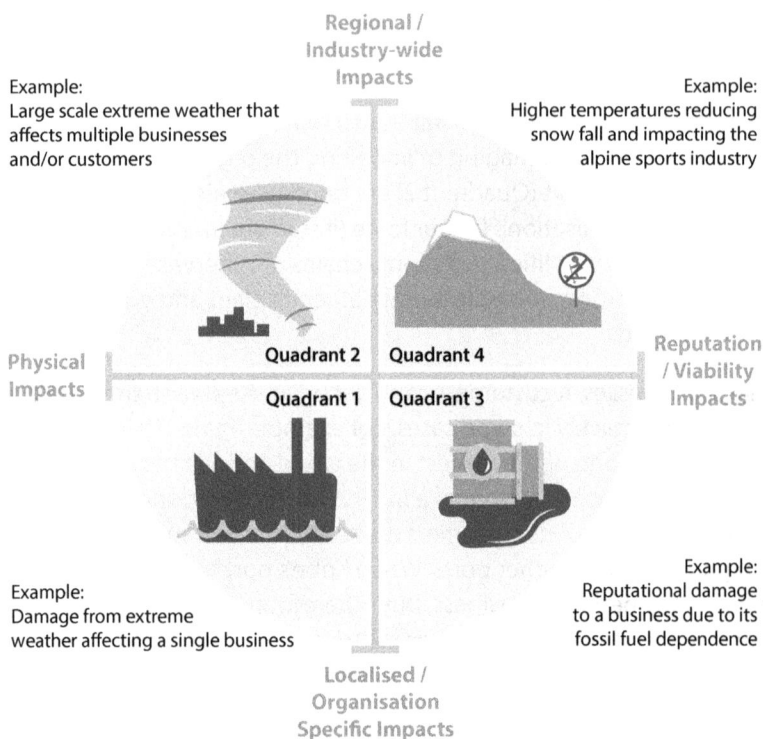

Regional /
Industry-wide
Impacts

Example:
Large scale extreme weather that
affects multiple businesses
and/or customers

Example:
Higher temperatures reducing
snow fall and impacting the
alpine sports industry

Physical
Impacts

Quadrant 2   Quadrant 4

Quadrant 1   Quadrant 3

Reputation
/ Viability
Impacts

Example:
Damage from extreme
weather affecting a single business

Example:
Reputational damage
to a business due to its
fossil fuel dependence

Localised /
Organisation
Specific Impacts

Figure 7 – Climate change impacts

Quardrant 3 risks include consumer backlash and/or regulation affecting demand for products or services. or rendering a product or process unviable. This is not necessarily an industry-wide phenomenon, since competitor organisations may have put in place measures to insulate them from these impacts such as avoiding price shocks associated with carbon pricing by reducing their supply chains' fossil fuel dependence.

Finally, Quadrant 4 considers community / societal / environmental disruption from climate or environmental impacts which renders an industry unviable. For example, wine production (or at least the ability to grow particular varieties to equivalent quality and productivity levels as today in many established regions) is likely to be a relatively early casualty due to the sensitive nature of grape growing.

In some cases significant impacts could be felt where the origins are quite abstracted from the organisation itself.

A simple example is firms that supply the fossil fuel industry, for example a business that installs oil and gas pipelines. Until recently, a lot of new projects required large scale / long haul pipeline infrastructure, particularly as oil and gas firms seek to exploit more marginally located fields.

During 2014 the price of oil dropped dramatically due to over-supply, and many exploration projects were put on hold, leading to downsizing and redundancies amongst pipeline firms.[xliii] If demand for fossil fuels also wanes, there will be less exploration, leading to less new fields to be exploited and therefore less need for new pipelines.

In a more benign example, companies providing, say, laundry or catering services to the hotel industry in a market that is dependent on coral coast tourism may need to seek an alternative customer base as the reefs decline.

Clearly there is a temporal dimension to the various impact quadrants, both in terms of when a firm might experience them; and also the potential lag between an adverse event and resultant negative consequences.

Weather related disasters (Quadrant 1 and 2 impacts) occur regularly and could affect any business at any time – with climate change both the probability of occurrence and the intensity of impacts are expected to increase in many regions.

Quadrant 3 risks are already occurring, with the major miners, oil companies, coal-fired electricity generators and banks among the primary targets.

It is expected that as regulation impacts the coal, oil and gas industry, a wider group of polluting industries will be actively targeted, potentially including the transportation sector, energy-intensive metal production, cement producers and so on.

As we have already seen, however, firms that are relatively benign can still be targeted through their business dealings with so-called "footprint negative" organisations. In the case of Quadrant 4, the marginalisation of some industries has already commenced, but in most cases significant impacts will not be seen for decades and for astute investors there is plenty of money to be made in the interim.

PART 2
OPPORTUNITY

"You can't sit on the lid of progress. If you do, you will be blown to pieces."

Henry J. Kaiser

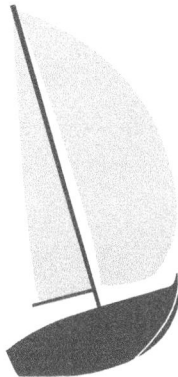

Chapter 3
A Cloud With a Silver Lining?

Wherever there is risk lies opportunity, and climate change is no different. The intriguingly named journalist McKenzie Funk, in his rollicking though sobering 2014 book Windfall: The Booming Business of Global Warming, tells the stories of a variety of speculators, both individuals and companies, who are staking an early claim within the Adaptive Economy. From the exploitation of newly accessible mineral deposits being revealed as Greenland's ice sheet recedes, to the fund managers who are buying up land in Siberia and along the upper Nile in Africa and the water-rights traders in the South Western United States and Australia, the people he meets are the vanguard of new ways of doing business.

Think of climate change as a market disruptor, much like the Internet or the motor car or telephone. These inventions created and transformed industries: catapulting some to success (road building, tyres, petrol stations and mechanics for example); while making others obsolete (the village smithy, messenger pigeon trainers and the steam locomotive).

While the previous section considered some of the disrupted industries, we will now look at the industries that may benefit from a changing climate.

These growth sectors relate to the four broad categories of goods and services our society will need in the coming decades – industries that will help with:

1. Mitigation, by reducing greenhouse emissions and broader environmental impacts;

2. Adaptation to the impacts of a changing climate;

3. Reversing the environmental degradation we have caused the planet; and

4. Engineering a more sustainable, steady state economy.

Some of these opportunities are already being exploited, but for smart companies there are still hundreds of products and services yet to be invented or areas where innovation will result in a competitive advantage and profit.

Depending on the opportunity, the financial impetus may come from several sources, including the carbon trading market (where credits can be purchased by polluters from projects that reduce emissions or sequester greenhouse gases), direct government spending, business-to-business private demand and consumer demand.

Public sector funding includes the United Nations' multi-billion dollar Green Climate Fund to assist developing countries with mitigation and adaptation,[xliv] and local initiatives such as the European Union's Climate-KIC (Knowledge Innovation Community) initiative, which provides incubator finance and support to develop entrepreneurial ideas to combat and adapt to climate change.[xlv] In the private sector a range of so-called Green Bonds and similar capital raising products have been launched, generating funds to support GHG mitigation projects.

How big is the prize? At the moment it's difficult to say, but the Adaptive Economy is emphatically a multi-trillion dollar per annum business prospect.

Renewable energy alone is currently an industry worth around US$250 billion per annum globally with expected growth to over US$1 trillion per annum as early as 2020.[xlvi]

Energy efficiency initiatives are already approaching half a trillion dollars per annum.[xlvii] And as we'll see in this section, that's just the low hanging fruit.

Massive new industries are likely to be spawned by the impetus behind the Adaptive Economy, filling an investment vacuum that will be caused by the decline of fossil fuels.

As increasing numbers of commentators are pointing out, the costs of adaptation to climate change potentially outweigh the costs of rapid mitigation. While some of the adaptations discussed in this section are subtle, each idea represents an opportunity for innovative and clear-thinking business people.

Chapter 4
The Mitigation Market

The word "mitigation" has been somewhat co-opted by climate change specialists to refer to the reduction or abatement of greenhouse gas emissions. This is what has been determined to be most critical to reducing the buildup of atmospheric greenhouse gas levels, therefore reducing the warming trend and associated climate changes.

Sources of emissions

Figure 8 shows the approximate global breakdown of sources of anthropogenic greenhouse gas emissions.

The data shows that electricity generation (via fossil-fuel burning power stations) is the single largest source of emissions, with the power mainly used in buildings (for heating, cooling, lighting, TVs, computers, cooking and so on) and by industrial processes.

Additional greenhouse gases are produced within buildings (for example, by oil or gas used for heating or cooking) and by industry (for example steel and cement production).

Transport, at 14% of emissions, covers road, rail, sea and air travel, almost all of which is dependent on burning diesel, petrol or other fossil fuels.

The category marked AFOLU refers to emissions associated with Agriculture, Forestry and Other Land Use changes. This is the main category, apart from some industrial processes, where emissions are created by means other than burning fossil fuels – in this case they come from releasing carbon from forests and soils into the atmosphere.

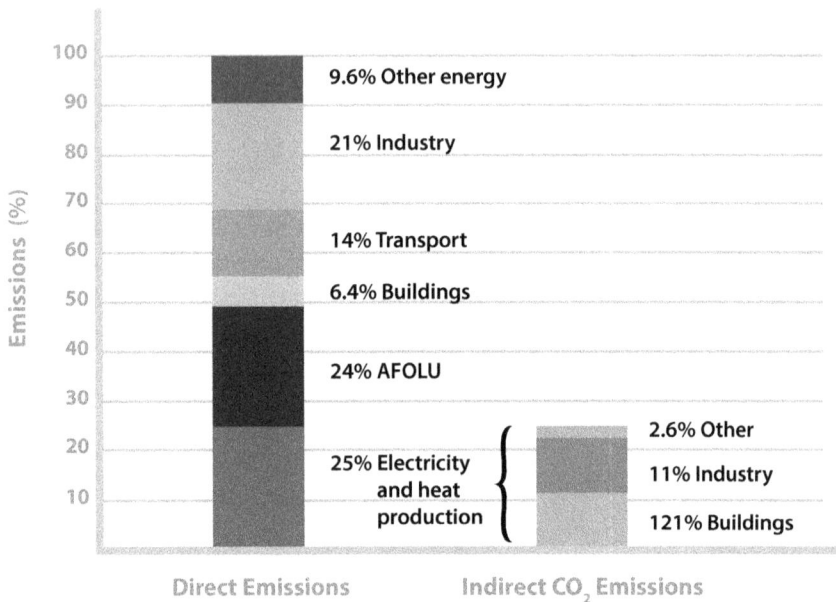

100

90

80

70 — Emissions (%)

60

50

40

30

20

10

9.6% Other energy

21% Industry

14% Transport

6.4% Buildings

24% AFOLU

25% Electricity
and heat
production

2.6% Other

11% Industry

121% Buildings

Direct Emissions   Indirect CO$_2$ Emissions

Figure 8 – Composition of anthropogenic GHG emissions[xlviii]

Of course, mitigation in an environmental context may also refer to reducing other activities that adversely impact on the environment including the depletion of fresh water supplies, creation of litter and waste, over-fishing and any other activity that disturbs natural eco systems.

In this section we'll examine opportunities for new products and services in the mitigation market, covering both greenhouse emission abatement and broader mitigation concepts.

Energy efficiency

The first step towards mitigation is typically through energy and resource efficiency: in other words, using less. And the efficiency market is booming, because in fiscally constrained times, cutting costs provides a good return on investment. It's simple maths – an extra dollar of revenue might only generate ten cents of profit, while a dollar of cost savings flows straight to the bottom line.

The most direct link between mitigation and efficiency is achieved through energy savings, since the vast majority of global energy use – including electricity generation, transportation, local heating and industrial – relies on burning fossil fuels and releases greenhouse gases and other pollutants.

Energy efficiency has been described as the low hanging fruit of GHG abatement because it can be literally as easy as turning off a light bulb. These kinds of simple, zero-cost behavioural measures can save a lot of power when multiplied across a country or the globe.

During the mid 2000's, several Australian state governments introduced a so-called "shadow price" on carbon emissions through the use of Energy Savings Certificates (in the state of New South Wales) and similar mechanisms, which enabled people who invested in energy-saving measures to recover some of their costs. This led to a number of schemes, such as private companies distributing packs of compact fluorescent light bulbs (CFLs) free to members of the public.

CFLs use about a fifth of the power of traditional incandescent bulbs to produce the same level of light, so the theory went that if consumers were incentivised to replace their incandescent bulbs, energy consumption would decline, therefore reducing emissions since most of NSW's power is generated from coal-fired plants.

It wasn't necessarily just about the environment, either – reducing individual consumers' energy use in a growing population defers the need to build additional power stations and the associated distribution infrastructure. It worked, and eventually Federal Government policy mandated the phase out of incandescent bulbs.

Roll forward five to ten years and CFLs are now being displaced by Light Emitting Diode (LED) technology, which offers a marginal further improvement in efficiency plus other benefits such as longevity, instant start (as opposed to CFLs, which generally need to warm up before achieving optimal brightness), no use of the toxin mercury, and less loss of luminance over the life of the globe.

Opportunity equals innovation and disruption

As with any new technology, the LED lighting market is in a flurry of innovation, with a variety of designs and standards fighting for prominence. Designs that can be retrofitted into existing incandescent, halogen or fluorescent fittings are in demand because this reduces the upfront costs. While the globes and tubes are still relatively expensive, growing economies of scale have seen prices decrease to the point of near price parity with less efficient alternatives at point of purchase, and a more competitive lifecycle price once longevity, energy-cost and maintenance are factored into the equation.

Other lighting industry firms have taken the idea of behavioural change as a route to efficiency and supplemented behaviour with technology. These innovations include lighting zones controlled by occupancy sensors: if there's nobody in a space, switch the lights off automatically. There is also the use of so-called "daylight harvesting", where around the perimeter of the building, if the levels of natural light coming in the windows are sufficient, lights can be automatically dimmed or switched off to save energy.

People are part of the equation

However, without clear communication to building occupants about how and why the lighting system works, trouble can arise. Daylight harvesting can cause changes to lighting levels, which may be distracting to occupants. Depending on how occupancy sensor zones are set up, people who are near the edge of a zone may lose some illumination if there is nobody in the adjacent zone and therefore its lights are switched off.

And at night, many people prefer the entire floor of their building to be well lit rather than just an island of light around their desk. Providing permanent lighting to exit paths is one way of overcoming this issue.

The take-away

There are a few key points we can draw from these examples:

1. New products and services, driven by the need to reduce costs and GHG emissions, are disrupting traditional technologies.

2. Innovators are profiting, while laggards who clung to incandescent and halogen lighting technologies have suffered.[xlix] For example, Osram, at one time the world's second largest lighting company by sales shed thousands of jobs and watched profits plummet as LED technology gathered momentum. However, the normal rules of market turbulence and consolidation apply as the number of players in the market is whittled down as de facto standards emerge.

3. Providing stepping-stones (such as LED lights that can be retrofitted to existing incandescent or fluorescent fittings) helps improve adoption and take up rates. It may be more efficient to have an LED light use a custom designed fitting, but most organisations and individuals would only consider that in the context of infrequent renovations rather than everyday operations.

4. Good technology (daylight harvesting and occupancy sensors) doesn't always win if the behavioural implications are not well thought through. The need for effective communication and management of change cannot be overstated.

Another key point is that incentives need to be aligned to promote uptake.

The split incentive dilemma

In Australia most organisations are tenants rather than owners of commercial buildings. Under conventional leasing arrangements, the tenant pays an electricity bill for energy used for lighting within the tenanted area. The landlord pays for the energy bill that covers lighting in lobbies, toilets and car parks, plus centralised heating and air conditioning systems and elevators, which is then passed on to the tenant in the form of an aggregated outgoings charge, which also includes maintenance, cleaning and management costs.

When businesses are comparing different buildings they will typically factor in the outgoings costs, so landlords are incentivised to upgrade lobby, toilet and car park lighting to reduce energy costs.

Unfortunately, the landlord generally owns and is responsible for the maintenance of the standard grid of lighting fixtures, bulbs/tubes and associated wiring that provides the lighting in the tenanted area. Therefore, the capital cost of lighting efficiency upgrades is borne by the landlord, but the benefit accrues to the tenant in the form of lower tenancy energy bills.

The landlord therefore has little incentive to upgrade tenant area lighting to improve energy efficiency, since they do not directly benefit. It has only been larger tenants for whom energy represents a material cost and who have some leverage with landlords that have in some cases made tenancy lighting upgrades a condition of moving into a new building or renewing a lease on their existing premises.

This issue of split incentives has therefore slowed the uptake of tenancy lighting efficiency improvements in the mid and lower tiers of the commercial property market, even though in many cases such projects have a payback period of two years or less.

However, a number of lighting companies are now teaming up with finance providers to offer a managed, leased lighting service. In this model the third party upgrades the tenancy lighting under an agreement that sees it own the lighting asset and be responsible for maintaining it over a multi-year period. The landlord avoids the upfront capital outlay, and instead has monthly operational costs that can be factored into outgoings charges to tenants, which are offset by reduced electricity costs due to the improved efficiency.

When comparing buildings, prospective tenants need to be astute enough to factor in the impact on their power bills and determine their total cost of occupation. But unless the landlord facilitates this process and actively sells the benefits of the lighting system, the arrangement could appear slightly more expensive than a comparative building where the light fittings have long been fully depreciated but the electricity consumption will be significantly higher.

Other opportunities in the efficiency space

Lighting is just one of the most obvious examples of profitable energy efficiency opportunities. There are dozens of others, including:

- More efficient heating, ventilation and air conditioning (HVAC) systems. From variable speed fans (which reduce energy consumption by spinning more slowly or not at all when they're not needed) to significant improvements in the performance of cooling and heating systems, to fuel switching for traditional oil based heating systems in cooler climate countries, there has been considerable innovation in the HVAC space.

- Building design that manages passive solar load and utilises natural ventilation to reduce or eliminate the need for artificial cooling and heating. This approach results in buildings that absorb the sun's warmth in winter and minimise the impact of its heat in summer. There are also building products that improve insulation and thermal massing, or others such as specialised high-performance glazing, convective roof fans and draught exclusion to stop heat leaking out in winter while minimising its intrusion during summer.

- Reducing the amount of power used by electrical appliances and computers when in standby mode (so-called "vampire power"). Apart from innovations within the devices themselves, smart new inventions have emerged such as power boards that switch off power to other devices (such as sound systems or gaming consoles) when a central device (generally the television) is put into standby mode. Another innovation is the central switch, also known as a "green switch" or "kill switch", which enables people to switch off the power to all non-essential equipment in their tenancy or home as they exit the front door.

- Water heating systems are saving energy and reducing emissions through various innovations including the use of timers.

- Cooking and refrigeration systems and other appliances are generally becoming more efficient.

- Energy efficiency improvements in vertical transportation (lifts and escalators) such as regenerative drive lifts.[10]

- Building management systems, sensors and controls that intelligently optimise energy use in buildings while providing real time reporting that allows facility managers to identify further opportunities to refine efficiency.

That's at the building level. Electricity efficiency improvements also abound in other sectors including mining, manufacturing, telecommunications and of course electricity generation itself.

---

10   These drives feed energy generated during braking cycles back into the building for use by other systems such as heating, ventilation, air conditioning and lighting.

Efficiency in IT

In the growing information technology sector there are huge opportunities to reign in energy waste, which has become profligate due to a phenomenon known as Moore's Law.

Postulated by Geoffrey Moore, one of the key figures in the development of silicon chips in the 1960s, it originally predicted that the number of transistors on a chip would roughly double every two years.[i] Fast forward nearly 50 years and Moore's Law has become a proxy for the regular doubling of computer power including processor, memory and storage capacity, generally at approximately the same price point. That's around 24 doublings since chips began, so if the capability of an original computer was baselined to one, today's computers are theoretically 8 million times more powerful.

Realising that next year's computers will be substantially faster than last year's, software developers who write the apps we use on our laptops, tablets and smart phones have become lazy about the efficiency of their code. Whereas the original space shuttle was said to run on about 420,000 lines of code for all its systems, recent versions of the Windows operating system have had 40 to 50 million. Let alone the applications that run on it. Rather than work on the assumption of minimal computing resources, many developers create software that performs passably on the current generation of machines but better on a brand new one.

A symbiotic relationship has developed between major hardware manufacturers and software developers. Whether they want new features or not, consumers are increasingly forced to upgrade their software to ensure continued support or gain access to security fixes. Newer versions of software often perform more poorly on the same computer than the previous version, so there is an incentive to upgrade the hardware. Most large organisations now reckon on upgrading their IT fleet about once every three years to ensure users maintain adequate performance.

Meanwhile mobile devices are often linked to two year data plans, at the end of which the user has the chance to upgrade for little additional cost. Many consumers enjoy the opportunity to have the latest or most fashionable device, even though there is rarely a substantive change between models that makes their previous device obsolete. And so the cycle of planned obsolescence and waste continues.

In recent years the hardware industry has started to clean up its act from an energy efficiency perspective, with newer devices requiring relatively less power per "compute operation per second" (be it megaflops or some other measure) than earlier iterations. However, the number of computing devices has continued to balloon, spurred by smart phones, tablets and the millions of apps requiring server power in unseen data centres.

While the software industry lacks effective efficiency standards, our use of information technology will continue to demand a greater share of global electricity demand.[li]

Of course, even with significantly better energy efficiency, the computer hardware makers cannot consider their operations "sustainable" given the vast amount of e-waste the constant upgrade cycle creates: literal mountains of plastic, glass, rare earths, toxic compounds and other materials wind up in landfill (or as litter) every year.

For example, LCD computer monitors do what they do in part because of fluorinated greenhouse gases (F-GHGs) such as Nitrogen Trifluoride, which has a global warming potential[11] 17,200 times that of carbon dioxide (that is, a kilogram of NF_3 being emitted into the atmosphere has the same warming impact of over 17 tonnes of carbon dioxide).[lii]

The disposable nature of IT equipment means that a lot of these types of gases are escaping into the atmosphere as superseded equipment is crushed in landfill. Indeed, man-made GHGs from TVs and monitors are routinely detected at the remote Cape Grim atmospheric monitoring station on the tip of Tasmania.[liii]

While it's not necessarily in the commercial interests of the information technology industry to ease up on the speed with which new versions of hardware and software are developed and released, and while the sector is not generally viewed as a climate demon (yet), the rate of obsolescence is unsustainable.

At some point governments could act to tax the industry in order to drive up prices and reduce demand. However, the industry itself could work collaboratively to recondition consumers to paying more for their devices and apps, on the grounds that they are expected to be more durable and will keep performing with successive versions of increasingly efficient software. Release

11   GWP – a measure of a gas's greenhouse effect relative to Carbon Dioxide.

cycles could be slowed down, which in itself would provide more time to develop the most efficient hardware and software.

Renewable energy

While energy efficiency reduces GHG emissions by cutting demand for power, the renewable energy sector reduces emissions by taking fossil fuels out of the equation.

Renewable energy generation encompasses a growing range of technologies including the traditional hydropower (which substitutes steam created by boiling water via burning fossil fuels to drive turbines, with a stream of water rushing downhill to drive a turbine) and wind (which converts wind energy to rotation to drive a turbine).

Solar power, on the other hand, is harnessed in two forms. Thermal solar has traditionally been used for water heating, simply by concentrating the sun's heat onto pipes carrying water. Translated to an industrial scale, thermal solar plants are now being established where thousands of mirrors focus the sun's rays onto what is effectively a boiler, which produces steam and (you guessed it) drives a turbine to produce electricity. On the other hand photo-voltaic solar panels use chemical processes to convert the sun's energy to electricity with no turbines involved.

There are also generation technologies harnessing energy from waves, tides, river currents (without necessarily needing to dam the river), geothermal heat or steam from inside the earth, and making use of chemical or kinetic energy.[liv]

The explosion of investment in the renewables sector has seen a flurry of innovation, driven at the top end of town by giant turbine specialists such as General Electric and Siemens, while dozens of start-ups have emerged from universities and other research teams.

The efficiency of photovoltaic panels in converting sunlight to electricity has increased markedly, along with techniques to integrate them more seamlessly into roofs, for example, replacing traditional roofing materials with solar-integrated tiles or panels, also exterior walls and even – somewhat improbably given the wear and tear considerations – road surfaces.[lv]

These advances, combined with the economies of scale now being seen, mean the cost of major forms of renewable generation are approaching or have passed so-called "grid parity". In other words, in some situations it is now cheaper to generate power from renewable sources rather than traditional coal, once capital and operating costs and relative plant longevity are taken into account.

The cost of renewable generation is largely front-loaded, since the ongoing "fuel" (the sun, wind or water) is free, whereas fossil fuel plants are subject to the vagaries of fuel and transport prices over a lifespan of around 50 years.[lvi]

Once a staple of the renewable energy sector, there is still a reasonable level of investment in hydropower. For example, a recent report identified over €EUR1.3 trillion worth of planned and potential investment in the sector in Europe alone.[lvii] In a climate changing world, however, many hydropower schemes may be at risk from declining river levels due to changes in rain and snow fall and declining glaciers, as well as competing demand for agricultural and environmental flows from dwindling supplies.

Wind and solar are sometimes criticised as not being suitable to provide an effective "base load" generation replacement for coal or oil power stations because the wind doesn't always blow and the sun doesn't always shine. Some proponents argue that installing such generation capacity over a wide area and connecting it through a centralised grid will overcome this challenge, though this implies considerable investment in redundancy. Others point out that wave and tidal flow generation methods provide scope for continuous generation, though so far there has only been limited investment in this area.

One option is to combine intermittent generation sources with power storage systems, otherwise known as batteries. Significant investment in electric vehicle (EV) technology is currently driving down the cost of battery arrays. For example, Tesla, a US-based company producing sporty and sophisticated EVs, has been building a multi-billion dollar factory in the US state of Nevada, which will produce 50 GWh worth of batteries per annum once at full production; enough, says the manufacturer, to power 500,000 of its cars.[lviii]

At the residential level it is expected that it will soon be possible for home owners to go "off grid" with rooftop solar panels and a battery storage system for much the same cost as getting their power from the local utility company (when upfront costs are amortised over the life of the system).

With Australian governments pulling back from the preferential feed-in tariffs that incentivised significant investment in roof top solar systems in the mid 2000s (by effectively providing a subsidy to home owners), affordable storage and the chance to permanently avoid ever-rising usage and network charges may help spur the next wave of rooftop solar investment. Indeed, in April 2015 Tesla announced its Power Wall product, aimed squarely at the domestic solar power storage market.

Another form of energy storage is seen in the form of large scale thermal solar installations where instead of heating water directly, the sun's energy is used to heat a chemical compound to much higher temperatures. These so-called "molten salts" can then be stored at high temperature for sustained periods and used to produce steam and in turn generate electricity overnight and on cloudy days. This emerging technology may be able to help solar replace coal and other fossil fuel plants for base load electricity generation.

Rethinking the grid

Localised generation and storage offers potential opportunities for the creation of so-called "micro-grids", where groups of businesses or households establish a local electricity network to share electricity and/or improve the reliability of individual systems.

For example, the City of Sydney, Australia, has been establishing a network of gas powered tri-generation plants.[lix] Gas is still a fossil fuel, but it is significantly less emissions intensive than coal. Not only do these tri-gen plants produce electricity to power city buildings, the process also creates surplus heat that can be used for heating buildings in winter and, through the use of an absorption chiller, the heat can also be used to create chilled water for connection to air conditioning systems in commercial buildings.

This optimises energy efficiency, while generating electricity close to the point of use reduces transmission losses. These can be significant, since power stations are often located over 100km from the point of use.

A variety of new technologies are required to support micro-grids, including suitably scaled systems for monitoring, metering, billing, maintenance and so on. Not to mention, in the case of tri-generation, the additional complexity of combining plumbing, heating and air conditioning into the mix.

The nuclear question – fission or fusion?

There is one form of power generation (although it's not renewable) that raises hackles for many people but may provide an effective compromise if base load generation needs cannot effectively be met from fully renewable forms such as wind and solar or waves and tides: nuclear.

Politicians, environmentalists and the public are polarised on the issue of nuclear power. On the one hand, nuclear reactors provide a steady base load generation and don't emit greenhouse gases. On the other, they remain vulnerable to dangerous radiation leaks through human failures or natural disasters, as seen in the cases of Chernobyl (Russia) and more recently Fukushima (Japan).

Their fuel, generally enriched Uranium or Plutonium, is the same stuff that atomic bombs are made from, so security becomes problematic, particularly for reactors located in geopolitically unstable regions or areas occupied by terrorist groups. And there's the controversial problem of nuclear waste disposal.

Currently there's a lot of interest in Thorium reactors. Thorium is more abundant than Uranium, less fuel is required for equivalent power output, the process does not require expensive enrichment before the fuel can be used, and it produces considerably less nuclear waste than conventional reactors. There are also potential advantages in the design and operation of the reactor. Thorium is also not suitable for nuclear weapons production, so some of the security problems are abated, though depending on the process used the waste may be closer to weapons grade.

Several countries have pilot programs in place to develop this technology, which ironically was investigated but abandoned during the Cold War era due to its lack of offensive capability.[ix]

In any case a renaissance in nuclear power would create many opportunities including fuel extraction and transportation, engineering and construction, waste disposal and safety monitoring.

But that's nuclear fission. The holy grail of energy production is nuclear fusion. Whereas fission splits atoms to release energy, but in so doing also releases lethal radiation, fusion joins atoms together to make heavier elements, creating vast amounts of heat energy but without the radiation.

In the Back to the Future films of the 1980s it was imagined that by 2015 we would all be driving fusion powered flying vehicles that could be refueled with a few scraps of waste food. Back in the present, efforts to create fusion power plants have been confounded by the challenge of safely containing the heat, which runs into millions of degrees.

In late 2014, however, aerospace and defence firm Lockheed Martin announced that it was working on a magnetic container and expected to have a working prototype fusion generator by 2017 that could be carried on the back of a truck.[lxi] If this turns out to be achievable it could become one of the greatest inventions of all time, allowing the production of unlimited clean and relatively cheap energy in a footprint that could be adapted for transportation as well as stationary energy.

Can coal be cleaned up?

The potential saviour of the coal-fired generation industry is a technology called carbon capture and storage (CCS), which aims to capture and trap carbon emissions from power stations underground where they can be sequestered safely and not emitted into the atmosphere. So far, attempts at CCS have met with limited success and at considerable cost. Various programs have been abandoned, including a United States government funded trial.[lxii]

The lack of an effective price on carbon emissions is one obstacle. However, if future developments can be proven and existing power stations retrofitted cost effectively, then coal could continue to be burned without creating GHG emissions, which could significantly reduce the cost of transforming the world's energy system to renewables and avoid mothballing trillions of dollars of potentially viable assets.

Emissions beyond electricity

While globally, electricity generation represents the largest single source of anthropogenic GHG emissions (around 25%), there are a number of other significant sources including:

- Industrial processes that lead to emissions independent of energy supply. For example, processes involved in cement and steel production result in high levels of GHG emissions.

- Land use, change in land use and forestry, particularly associated with deforestation, burning of forests, other land clearing and the decay of peat soils (the process of which releases GHGs).

- Agriculture, both through poor soil management, methane-emitting livestock (the numbers of which have soared as economic conditions have allowed more people to afford to eat meat) and the burning of biomass.

- Transportation, given the predominant use of petrol, diesel and other fossil fuels by road, rail, air and marine vehicles.

- Buildings (excluding externally generated electricity use), mainly covering on-site burning of fossil fuels (typically gas and heating oil) for space and water heating and cooking.

- Waste and wastewater. Our trash mountain releases methane as it breaks down in landfill, along with the emission of other GHGs such as nitrous oxide.

It is beyond the scope of this book to investigate mitigation opportunities in all these sectors, but suffice to say there are many technologies and processes that can be innovated to reduce GHG emissions.

In some cases processes or products that are GHG-intensive may be replaced by substitutes with lesser environmental impacts, adversely impacting one sector to the advantage of another. In other cases there will be improvements within the sector itself, creating competitive advantage for producers that are early adopters.

Auto manufacturers embracing the innovation imperative

In the transportation sector, for example, incremental improvements might include road surfaces and tyre designs that can increase or decrease friction and improve vehicle efficiency. Other innovations have included aerodynamic efficiency, improved engine design, electronic engine management, hybrid designs such as the Toyota Prius that use braking and downhill energy to charge batteries supporting an electric engine that supplements the petrol engine, and pure electric vehicles (EVs), which, when charged from renewable energy sources are effectively emissions free.

This is where the focus shifts from incremental to disruptive innovation, in this case involving the replacement of the fossil fuel powered (petrol or diesel) internal combustion engine. For example, research has found that even when charged from electricity sourced from coal-fired plants, EVs still out-perform many conventional combustion engines when the relative emissions are taken into account.[lxiii]

EVs are also quieter, produce less local air pollution, and as pioneer EV manufacturer Tesla has demonstrated can provide reasonable range between charges (currently over 400km and improving). They are also a lot of fun to drive. The main disadvantage is recharge time (still measured in multiple hours though Tesla's Supercharging stations can deliver around a two-thirds top up in about half an hour), and the current lack of availability of public charging points in many locations. The commercialisation of recently discovered grapheme could change that, promising a quantum improvement in battery charging times and stored energy to weight ratios. Coincidentally it could also double the efficiency of solar panels, meaning it may be one of the most critical discoveries in terms of transitioning to wholesale use of renewables.[lxiv]

To compensate for current concerns about range and charging time, several manufacturers have recently released EVs that also have a conventional petrol engine to provide extra range and the comfort of knowing that they can be refueled easily when travelling long distances. While this sounds similar to the hybrid concept, the difference is that it is possible to run the car exclusively on the battery until it is discharged.

Flow-on effects – even more innovation

A parallel emerging technology involves vehicles based on hydrogen fuel cells, with major manufacturers poised to release commercially available models in the near future. A fuel cell converts hydrogen to electrical energy using a chemical reaction (not combustion), which charges a battery (smaller than the one in an EV), which in turn drives an electric motor, producing only water as a by-product.

However, although hydrogen is the most abundant element, it first needs to be extracted from another molecule – generally natural gas. This process is energy intensive and subsequently requires the hydrogen be stored under pressure and transported to fuelling stations. All these steps may produce GHG emissions.

At the time of writing about the only hydrogen fuelling infrastructure in the world consists of a handful of stations in California, so conventional petrol stations would need to be modified – a costly and time consuming process to achieve the necessary scale.

Conversely, electricity is already reticulated almost everywhere, meaning EVs can be rolled out at scale today, particularly for urban applications. And the potential energy in the hydrogen suffers from similar levels of "generation and transmission" losses compared to electricity production and generation: at the end of the process, as little as 25% of the energy is actually converted to electricity to power the vehicle.[12] While EV batteries degrade over time and need to be replaced, so does the hydrogen fuel cell.

In short it is difficult to see hydrogen fuel cell vehicles leap-frogging EVs unless, as in the case of VHS video recorders vs Betamax (a superior technology), the industry heavyweights decide (by superior marketing and rapid infrastructure deployment) that hydrogen fuel cell cars are to be the way of the future.

Autonomous vehicles, such as Google's self-driving car, are another innovation to watch. If such vehicles were to achieve substantial market penetration, driving could become quicker, safer and significantly more efficient. Driving software could improve the efficiency of individual vehicles: avoiding rapid acceleration and braking or high speeds where fuel efficiency decreases rapidly; minimising energy consumption while idle (which is very easy to do with an electric vehicle); and so on.

And if autonomous vehicles should be networked and linked to city traffic telemetry systems, even greater energy efficiency improvements could be made. Journey times could be slashed as the vehicle network reduces traffic congestion and associated fuel inefficiency. Software could ensure vehicles merge lanes smoothly; depart on cue from traffic lights; tune traffic light

---

12 Electricity generation losses depend on the method, with coal burning steam turbines wasting perhaps up to 50% of the calorific – or energy – content of the coal, compared to only a few percent in the case of hydro-electric generation. Transmission losses are generally estimated at up to 10%.[lxv] In the case of EVs, the inefficiency of the batteries in converting and storing energy from the grid also needs to be taken into account, but on balance total losses (generation fuel to "power at the wheels") have been estimated by a US government agency at around 60%.[lxvi]

sequences in real time based on vehicle volumes; and optimise routes to avoid traffic snarls.

When two or more self-driving cars are in convoy, following distances between them could be minimised, reducing the amount of road occupied by each vehicle and therefore increasing road capacity.

On the other hand, auto smash repairers and emergency wards could lose business as the accident rate decreases, since the computer can be programmed to drive defensively and to the letter of the law. This would minimise crashes as a result of speeding, concentration lapses or of course from alcohol affected drivers.

When scouting for opportunity in the automotive sector, a key question is whether new entrants with disruptive technologies can displace the giants with their massive scale advantages.

Many of the majors have dabbled with EV and fuel cell technologies for many years and have significant capability to push them out at scale if they sense that the timing is right. A Toyota or GM acting almost unilaterally could swamp the likes of Tesla, grabbing the all-important mid-market and sending would-be upstarts back to the high end hobbyist market.

Nevertheless, there are likely to be opportunities for suppliers to the automotive industry that can deliver innovations that reduce production costs, improve range or longevity and so on, for whichever technology emerges as the dominant replacement to the internal combustion engine.

Autonomous vehicles may also threaten overall vehicle sales, since they lend themselves to shared use or ownership structures. The Australian pioneer in vehicle sharing, GoGet, has demonstrated that it is possible to enjoy many of the benefits of car ownership for central city dwellers without most of the hassles (high fixed costs, parking, servicing and so on).

Replace that fleet with self driving cars that literally pick you up curb-side when you need them, and that would tempt a much greater number of households into abandoning car ownership. It would also threaten the market share of traditional taxi services.

No wonder, then, it's a technology firm rather than traditional auto manufacturer spearheading the autonomous vehicle movement. Google can potentially benefit from freeing people up from driving by offering superior in-car entertainment and web services. To the extent this leads to a decline in car sales, the environment benefits from reduced embodied emissions, other pollution and resource use.

Meanwhile, while they may never be a dominant form of transport in most cities, bicycle commuting is enjoying a growth curve, with a number of municipal authorities investing in the construction of dedicated bike lanes and other initiatives to encourage cyclists onto the road as an alternative to private cars.

In addition to construction infrastructure firms, other beneficiaries of this trend include bicycle manufacturers, retailers, repairers, and suppliers of related cyclist paraphernalia, and the subsidiary fitness benefits can potentially ease some of the strain on the health system.[lxvii]

Public transport is another area that is ripe for development in many cities to reduce road congestion and improve fuel efficiency. The carbon footprint of an individual on a reasonably full bus, tram or train is vastly reduced compared to the same person driving an SUV (or even a small efficient car) to work. Improving the commuter attractiveness of buses through the construction of dedicated bus-ways, which can significantly reduce commute times, in conjunction with convenient timetables, routes, smart ticketing and low fares is helping to reduce transport emissions.

High speed rail is also undergoing a renaissance in many countries, with governments seeing efficiency and other benefits over road haulage for inter-city goods transportation; and a much less greenhouse gas-intensive option for shifting people compared to flying.

When inter-city travellers on high speed rail weigh up the time efficiencies associated with central city station locations and minimal check-in formalities compared to airports that are generally on city outskirts, door-to-door journey times can be comparable for journeys up to around 600km.[lxviii]

Finally, aircraft manufacturers are experimenting with biomimicry,[lxix] forming flexible wing structures that can be reshaped in flight, minimising the fuel-inefficient drag associated with mechanically separate flaps. Current designs have stripped weight using carbon fibre and other lighter materials. Air traffic controllers are working with airlines to develop more fuel efficient routes, taking advantages of high altitude tail winds and minimising the need for aircraft to circle before landing.

Chapter 5
How Do We Need to Adapt?

From Part 1 we know that climate change brings with it a wide array of changes to the weather, sea levels, ocean acidity levels, societal attitudes towards certain types of activities, and so on. In searching for opportunity amongst the changes we've found it's worthwhile looking at things from the point of view of basic needs, such as:

- What will we drink?

- What will we eat?

- Where will we live?

- How will we get around?[13]

- What will we buy?

- How will we stay healthy?

- How will we protect and defend ourselves?

- What will we do?

As we saw in Chapter 1 there are both geographical and temporal dimensions to these concepts. Different locations will have different needs and in many cases these needs will change as time passes and the multi-faceted impacts of climate change become more acute.

For example, while initially it may be acceptable to build sea walls to defend coastal property and infrastructure from the storm surges that will be magnified by more intense extreme weather events and sea level rise, at some point (in most cases still decades hence) it will become impractical or unaffordable to do so. The strategy will change to "abandon and retreat".

In Sydney Australia, a global city blessed with dozens of beautiful beaches, the Pacific Ocean's encroachment and eventual inundation of those beaches will change the nature of coastal living. Beachfront suburbs will no longer carry such a price premium when the beach has gone, regardless of whether the

---

13   A range of potential adaptations in the transport sector are addressed in the previous chapter.

homes are still out of harm's way. Premium property will be defined in terms of higher ground suburbs featuring transportation corridors that do not pass near sea level.

On the non-seaward edges of the city, the expected increasing frequency and ferocity of bush fires may also dampen values. New construction codes introduced in the wake of the deadly 2009 Victorian bush fires significantly increase the cost of building and renovating in bushfire prone land, while insurance in such areas can also be more expensive.

Similarly, some commentators claim that increased concentration of atmospheric CO_2 will promote higher growth rates amongst agricultural crops (not to mention invasive weed species) and some regions at higher latitude may benefit from warming, enabling them to be used for agricultural production for the first time.

However, many scientists dispute such assertions, pointing out that the disadvantages associated with increasing average temperatures, greater frequency of extreme temperatures, and particularly greater variability of precipitation will combine to outweigh any benefits associated with CO_2 concentrations. As well as CO_2, good soil, a steady water supply and some warmth, plants need adequate sunlight to grow – that is what drives photosynthesis – and there's simply less sunlight at higher latitudes due to the curve of the earth.

What will we drink?

Fresh water is fundamental for survival, not just for human physiology, but also for the plant and animal crops we eat and the natural environments we interact with. It is also used in the extraction of coal and other fossil fuels, and for a range of energy production and industrial uses. Water is currently critical to a majority of commercial building air conditioning systems, with evaporative cooling towers still a popular heat exchange mechanism.

As noted earlier, various issues are threatening the consistent supply of fresh water where it's needed, including:

- Variability in patterns of precipitation in some areas. While over a long enough period rain gauges may register much the same levels, rainfall might become more concentrated, leading to longer droughts and more intense storms. In the latter case, flood waters can destroy crops and erode soils, and less water is absorbed into the land overall. Around the globe, crippling droughts are becoming more common, reducing agricultural production and in some cases leading to erratic supplies in some of the world's largest cities. Even Brazil – which boasts the largest river systems in the world – is not immune, with supply disrupted in early 2015 to parts of Sao Paulo, a city with a metropolitan population of over 20 million people.[lxx]

- Shifting rainfall patterns that make traditionally wetter areas even more so, and drier ones more parched.

- Reduced natural water storage (in the form of snow packs and glaciers) resulting in declining river flows during summer.

- Warmer temperatures leading to higher evaporation rates, reducing the moisture content of soils.

- Deforestation reducing the sponge-like ability of forests to absorb water and release it gradually into water catchments, further aggravating the increasing "feast or famine" trend.

- Upstream users disrupting the natural flow of rivers by extracting too much water for irrigation, urban water supplies, hydro electricity generation and other uses. Population growth also means many river systems and catchments are under significant strain.

- Sea level rise leading to the incursion of salt water into fresh water sources used in low lying coastal areas.

Supply and efficiency

These changes present a range of opportunities for innovation, starting with water efficiency: if there's less water to go around in a given location, we'll need to use it more carefully. There are dozens of ways this can be achieved including:

- The introduction of water meters and direct usage charges, which have still not been implemented in many parts of the world. Internet-connected smart water meters, which can remind building occupants that they've left a tap running or that their use is trending upwards could gain a ready market, much like smart electricity meters (combined with high energy prices) have begun to transform consumers' power usage.

- Advances in tapware, toilets and other plumbing fittings to reduce consumption and waste. Shower timers are another mechanism that can help with behavioural change.

- On-site storage of rainwater collected from roofs and so-called grey-water recycling systems (which re-use waste water from washing machines, bath and shower discharge) are reducing the amount of potable water that is used for watering gardens or flushing toilets. Rain water can also be used to supply washing machines or for other uses where drinking-quality water is not required. In some cases such schemes have been implemented at a suburban level, typically where infrastructure for new developments is being put in place.

- Redesigning industrial processes to use less water and/or make greater use of recycled waste water.

- Repairing/replacing ageing water reticulation networks to reduce leakage.

As water supplies are increasingly stressed, governments must seek alternate supplies – or face abandoning towns in marginal locations. It is logical to expect there will continue to be considerable investment in coastal desalination plants and new networks to carry fresh water to both urban and rural users.

A disadvantage of desalination is the exposure of the plant's coastal sites to sea level rise and storm surges. Indeed, some existing plants may need to be relocated to higher ground in time. Desalination is also an expensive and energy intensive process, so such projects should be combined with local renewable energy projects, such as wave or tidal generation if appropriate. While new desalination processes are emerging, which are considerably more energy efficient, the issue of what to do with the salty brine by-product remains an environmental challenge for many plants.

Alternatively the exploration and exploitation of fresh water from recently discovered submarine aquifers laid down off our coastlines during previous ice ages may well become a growing – though eventually finite – industry.[lxxi]

Whereas cities such as London in the United Kingdom and those lining the Mississippi River in the United States have long relied on river water that has had sewage discharged into it from communities upstream, the debate about water recycling has raged in even relatively water poor cities such as Sydney. Nevertheless, Singapore is now supplementing its water storage lake with highly treated waste water (i.e. sewage) meeting 30% of supply[lxxii] and in Perth,

Western Australia, recycled water is injected into the city's aquifer where it is drawn out again mixed with the groundwater as "new" water to bolster potable supplies.

As persistent droughts occur with greater frequency, more cities will be forced to – as one might euphemistically put it – drink their own champagne. Depending on the circumstances, water recycling may be a more cost effective option than desalination.[lxxiii] This will present many opportunities for providers of water treatment infrastructure, research into new forms of water treatment and purification and savvy marketers who can help consumers get over the "yuck factor".

In agricultural hinterlands far from the coast, new inventions may yield methods of "harvesting" water from the environment or atmosphere. Whereas in the past professional rain makers have attempted to stimulate precipitation by seeding likely looking clouds with silver iodide crystals (with often limited success), in the future biomimicry technologies could unlock new, energy and cost efficient ways of extracting and condensing water vapour from the air – provided the local humidity level is not too low.

There are already examples of what are essentially up-scaled dehumidifiers, which condense fresh water from the atmosphere but are fairly energy intensive (for example, SkyWell[lxxiv]).

At a more technologically simplistic level, rainwater falling on paved rural roadways could potentially be captured via drains, stored in buried cisterns installed at regular intervals and supplied to surrounding farms for irrigation uses via solar powered pumping stations.

Realising the potential of such innovations will create opportunities for meter makers, pipe layers, pump manufacturers, construction companies, engineers and a range of other industries.

Meanwhile, in the face of declining river flows, measures will need to be taken to ensure that irrigation uses are as efficient as possible (minimum waste / maximum benefit) and water rights markets will expand to more river systems, creating opportunities for exchange providers, traders and enforcement.

Water issues are also facing small island nations and low lying coastal areas on the mainland, where rising sea levels and storm surges are contaminating fresh groundwater sources. Cost-effective innovations to protect fresh water supplies will be highly sought after in such areas.

Transformation in bottled beverages

Another area in need of transformation is the bottled beverage market, starting with bottled water. In most developed countries tap water is perfectly safe to drink and tastes fine. Yet in the United States over 31 billion litres of bottled water was sold in 2006, approximately equivalent to one 300ml bottle per day for every person. Less than 1 in 4 bottles is recycled in the US. It has been estimated that one litre of bottled water requires an additional two litres of water in the production process, plus energy, oil and other materials to make the mostly plastic bottles, significant transportation emissions (water is heavy) and additional energy for refrigeration.[lxxv] And many consumers are willing to pay almost 2000 times more for something that can be accessed for a fraction of the cost and environmental impact, simply by turning on a tap.[14]

A small but growing number of communities have banned or discouraged the sale of bottled water and are implementing a future where residents and visitors fill reusable containers from free filtered water dispensers in streets and parks, creating opportunities for the sale, installation and maintenance of such kiosks.

Refrigerated filtered water taps are now standard in most new office building kitchens, displacing businesses involved in the delivery of five gallon water flagons to the once ubiquitous water coolers, and there is significant opportunity in the growing domestic market for consumers who dislike the taste of their local tap water or are suspicious about its origins. This demand will only increase as municipal utilities are forced to add recycled water to the mix.

Then there is the flavoured and carbonated beverage market, dominated by giants such as Coke and Pepsi and responsible for water and energy usage well surpassing the bottled water industry, due to the additional ingredients and associated processing overheads. While consumers are not going to abandon such brands anytime soon and nor will regulators make any serious attempt to limit their sale, there are alternatives presenting business opportunities.

---

14   While tap water is far less environmentally impactful compared to bottled, municipal water and waste water utilities use significant energy for pumping and filtration. For example, the US Environmental Protection Agency has estimated they account for 3-4% of total energy consumption in that country. It also believes significant energy efficiency savings (not to mention water savings from fixing ageing infrastrucutre) can be made with short payback periods, representing further opportunities for a variety of specialists.[lxxvi]

Seventies household icon Soda Stream, the do-it-yourself fizzy drink machine that combines tap water, drink syrup and (somewhat ironically) a bottle of compressed carbon dioxide, has made a remarkable comeback in recent years pushing itself as a more environmentally sensitive alternative to bottled carbonated beverages.[lxxvii] Meanwhile several manufacturers of in-home water purifiers have introduced carbonated modules, allowing consumers to dispense sparkling water straight from the tap.

For beverages that remain in containers, the question of which material is best – typically a choice between aluminium cans, glass, Tetrapak or plastic PET bottles – may create opportunities for certain container manufacturers to the detriment of others.

Perhaps surprisingly, some academic studies suggest PET edges out glass and aluminium in terms of its environmental impact, due to the significantly lower weight and embodied energy content, but offset by its lower recyclability.[lxxviii] On the other hand, plastic bottles are relatively porous to oxygen, meaning wine oxidises (goes bad) and beer or soft drinks go flat faster than glass or other alternatives. Glass is also superior for preserving the taste of a beverage, while green or brown bottle colouring can assist with protecting beverages from sunlight, something that can be done with plastic, but at the cost of recyclability.

A key byproduct of the bottled beverage market is litter, with many billions of plastic, glass and aluminium containers discarded or, at best, congesting landfill. Container recycling rates are still relatively low in many parts of the developed and developing world and in response a number of governments are adopting container deposit schemes (CDS).

Though fiercely resisted by the beverage industry (since a CDS raises the price of their wares relative to substitutes), various long standing schemes such as that in the state of South Australia have demonstrated substantial increases in container recycling rates and decreases in littering.[lxxix] For example, containers are estimated to account for around one in twelve items of litter in South Australia, versus approximately one in three items or 33% in the state of New South Wales, which has just anounced a CDS.[lxxx]

As governments introduce CDS or similar schemes, opportunities exist for providers of so-called reverse vending machines for returned containers; the additional infrastructure associated with the recovery, recycling and/or reuse of returned bottles; and firms who can create cash by collecting discarded containers and claiming the deposit refund. In the small market of South Australia (population 1.67 million), 10 cent deposit refunds totaling over A$58 million were paid in 2014.

What will we eat?

If providing enough water for agricultural and personal uses is becoming problematic, then ensuring adequate food supplies is potentially even more of a challenge.

Temperature rise associated with climate change is meaning warmer temperatures are moving pole-wards. Recent studies have suggested the tropical zone is expanding both North and South of the Equator at a rate of around 10km per year – significantly faster than many species can migrate by natural means.[lxxxi] Meanwhile, local weather is increasingly oscillating between extremes of drought, very high temperatures, intense storms and flooding rains, all of which lead to crop losses and/or depleted soils. While some common crops grow well within a reasonably broad temperature range (up to 25 degrees Celsius,[lxxxii] others are more selective, and many perform poorly when dealing with extremely hot days, the frequency of which is likely to increase in many growing regions.

Livestock face similar challenges, with significant mortality and reduced productivity associated with heat stress, plus the difficulty and expense of watering and feeding animals in drought affected areas and preventing them from drowning during floods.[lxxxiii] On top of that are the reputational issues the industry is experiencing due to the relatively high GHG emissions (including methane) associated with livestock, particularly cattle, with climate change campaigners urging consumers to eat less meat as part of personal mitigation efforts.

Not only is it going to get harder to produce food, we will also have more mouths to feed given increasing population growth over the next 30 years.

With this background, where do the business opportunities lie? Major trends in agriculture and food production are expected to include:

- Increased research and development of techniques to improve agricultural yields, particularly in the face of climatic changes, depleted soils and rising populations.

- A push to substitute crops and livestock associated with high water consumption and GHG emissions (or low yield per hectare) with alternatives that have reduced environmental impact.

- As a corollary to the previous point, innovation to reduce the GHG intensity of livestock is likely to be fertile ground (such as recent trials using feedstock additives to reduce ruminant methane emissions[lxxxiv]).

- Development of synthetic alternatives to farm-grown proteins.

- Measures to substitute synthetic nitrogen and phosphorus-based fertilisers for natural alternatives that have less adverse environmental impacts.

- Exploitation of newly accessible agricultural zones and marginalisation of others.

- Use of farmland as a carbon-sink through the introduction of techniques to minimise agricultural emissions and in some cases trap carbon in soils.

- Additional research, supply chain and behavioural change focused on reducing the current massive rates of food waste.

- Growing consumer demand for localised food production opening up new markets for innovative "urban farming" garden products including roof-based systems and productive green walls.

- Efforts to improve the sustainability and reduce the environmental impact of fisheries.

Increasing yields

Whereas the Green Revolution during the twentieth century relied mainly on the use of synthetic fertilisers and pesticides, the ability to feed up to 10 billion people (while also attempting to raise the living standards in developing nations – meaning greater food and meat consumption – and the same time addressing climate forces that will reduce agricultural productivity) will necessitate a new revolution, most likely involving genetically modified (GM) crops and livestock.[lxxxv] Not only will these crops need to withstand the harsher weather, they will also need modification to ward off fungal infestations such as blight or rust (after flooding rains) and insect pests. Simultaneously they will also need to deliver higher yields within the constraints of what in some areas will be a decreasing arable land area as existing farms give way to cities or – perhaps optimistically – newly planted forests.

Genetic modification of plants and animals is a highly contentious topic, with a range of scientific, ethical, religious and sometimes simply irrational arguments raised about potential risks. One argument that perhaps has substance is that the costs of GM research and development are high, meaning much of the resultant intellectual property will accrue to large multi nationals, who will then control the prices of GM seeds.

This may exacerbate the current inequalities around access to reliable food supplies at affordable prices. Nevertheless, just as the inhabitants of many cities have or are going to have to get past a phobia of recycled water supplies, so too are we going to have to embrace GM food. This opens up opportunities for governments to contribute a higher share of funding research programs than is currently the case, so that smaller players, including non-profits, can have a stake in the benefits.

Meat alternatives

With population and affluence generally increasing, another key area of research and product development will be focused around meat substitutes.

According to the UN Food and Agriculture Organisation's data, in 2012 around 38% of the earth's land area was given over to agricultural production, 31% was forest and the remaining 31% comprised barren land, urban areas, highways, mines and other sundry uses. Yet somehow, we will probably have to find a way to increase productive agricultural land by about 18% over the next 35 years to accommodate the nutritional demands of our growing population.

One solution will be to eat less meat, as currently, two thirds of the world's farmland is used for pasture or grazing for livestock, and part of the remaining one third which is cropland is actually growing food for edible animals, not people.[lxxxvi] There has been much written about the deleterious environmental consequences – including high water consumption and GHG emissions – of a diet rich in red meat (particularly beef). If we are to continue to meet a cultural desire to consume meat as a key part of our diet, then something has to give.

In 2013 a team of researchers funded by Google's Sergey Brin made headlines when they produced a burger patty from synthetically cultured beef protein grown from stem cells extracted from a pair of cows. Billed as the world's priciest burger (the project was reported to have cost €250,000), it was an important proof of the concept for cultured meat.[lxxxvii]

If produced at commercial scale, it is estimated that such meat, kilo for kilo, could reduce land and water use by 90%, energy use by 70% as well as significantly reducing greenhouse gas emissions (particularly the methane produced by belching cattle).

This experiment marks the beginning of a new product category with a brand new multi-faceted industry needed to realize it. Perhaps one day this will culminate in a new generation of food processors, such as those once envisaged by a generation of science fiction writers, allowing people to culture the synthetic meat of their choice at home.

The industry will also need an evangelical marketing campaign to convince people of the benefits and allay their concerns about potential risks, particularly in the early days before the finer points of texture and taste are worked out. Not to mention some charismatic chefs to teach people how to do delicious things with it.

Forecasting and crop protection

Given increasing seasonal and regional variability, the need for accurate rural weather forecasting will become more acute. Farmers will need predictions at a reasonably granular geographic scale incorporating long-term trends for persistent heat and drought conditions plus as much localised warning of specific extreme events as possible.

Weather futures and other financial derivatives are also emerging as ways that producers can hedge or insure against crop losses. And the benefits of accurate weather forecasting are not limited to agriculture. Fashion retailers are turning to sophisticated forecasting and analytics services such as Planalytics to support decisions about product range and stock levels. With the right data, firms whose sales are correlated with local weather conditions can anticipate demand and stock accordingly.

Protection of crops and livestock from weather extremes will also become critical. Innovation could feature monitoring systems for animals via GPS collars that track both location and potentially vital signs such as body temperature, hydration and blood sugar. These could help farmers optimise land use including the position of water points, keep animals well nourished, reduce the incidence of heat stress, and move herds away from low lying areas if floods threaten.

Just as horticulturalists cover crops with netting to keep off birds and in some cases insects, it may be that reflective mesh will be applied to keep crops cooler in the searing heat. It will also be important to provide shade for livestock (in the absence of trees) and appropriate ventilation or cooling of indoor piggeries and poultry farms. Horticultural crops such as bananas will need to be protected from cyclonic winds.

Land use management

As carbon and water rights trading systems become more sophisticated at a regulatory level, the use of land in different regions for specific crops and livestock is likely to come under greater scrutiny. The process of deciding what to plant or rear on a particular farm given its unique soil characteristics, temperature and rainfall patterns and runoff implications is likely to become more systematic, with analytic applications (and in certain cases government regulation) guiding farmers.

Australia's future as a major rice producer, for example, may need review as the variability of rainfall and river levels increases. A number of its wine growing regions are also threatened, with predicted climate change threatening the quality of its famous full bodied reds.[lxxxviii]

If today's agricultural zones are not necessarily going to be appropriate, then what are the opportunities involved in a migration of agricultural growing zones?

Well, land ownership for one thing. Other commentators such as McKenzie Funk have already noted long term speculators are snapping up large tracts of land in areas that are expected to become more fertile, particularly in northern Russia and Canada.

Large scale agriculture also needs infrastructure including irrigation, transportation, support services and produce/livestock markets and these will be required in some locations that have been previously undeveloped, Northern Australia potentially included.

Fertiliser and organics

Over-use of artificial fertiliser is a significant environmental issue we will return to in the next chapter. Use of alternatives is likely to increase. For example, planting off-season or rotational cover crops such as legumes can have benefits both in terms of fixing nitrogen in the soil, reducing the use of some herbicides and pesticides (since some cover crops repel certain pests), improving the organic content of the soil, reducing erosion and improving biodiversity.[lxxxix] Other substitutes include animal manure and even partially treated human sewage.[xc] Genetic engineering could also improve the uptake of nitrogen by cropping plants and reduce the level of chemically-derived additional nitrogen they need, therefore reducing the overall level of fertiliser required.[xci]

While the organic food industry is booming – worth around US$27 billion in 2010 in the US alone – and it reduces environmental issues associated with use of artificial fertiliser and pesticides, studies have found that crop yields are consistently lower than those of industrial agriculture.

In some cases these are relatively small differences (5% for beans and fruit trees, for example), but for most carbohydrate-based cereals and vegetables industrial methods lead to yields that are over 25% higher than organics.[xcii] That's significant in terms of assessing the opportunity cost of agricultural land against competing uses such as cultivating biofuels to replace aviation fuels and diesel for freight transportation, forestry, recreational and habitat uses such as wilderness areas and nature reserves.

There is scope to develop land assessment services to help planners, land owners and farmers determine the most effective and least environmentally degrading uses given climate, soil quality, water availability, eco-system conditions and anticipated demand factors.

Clearly, given more mouths to feed and growing per-capita demand, there will need to be intensive scrutiny in future to ensure agricultural output is optimised when the natural capital impacts such as loss of water, erosion, methane emissions, soil nutrient depletion and habitat loss are taken into account.

Carbon farming

Farming techniques also need to undergo a revolution to minimise the amount of greenhouse emissions released and improve the soil's ability to sequester carbon.

A new industry is developing around the concept of "carbon farming". Its practitioners adopt a number of techniques, the benefits of which are said to include: "carbon sequestration, reduced erosion and soil loss, improved soil structure, increased soil fertility, reduced soil salinity, healthier soils, vegetation and animals, increased biodiversity, buffering against drought and greater water efficiency", according to Carbon Farmers of Australia.[xciii] Carbon farmers can adopt a growing list of techniques including:

- maximising groundcover (minimal bare earth)
- grazing management
- no-till cropping
- pasture cropping
- mulching
- green manure
- stubble retention
- cover cropping
- exhaust injection
- controlled traffic
- precision application (fertiliser)
- natural fertilisers
- soil inoculants (probiotics)
- soil stimulants
- compost
- compost teas

While some of these innovations are up to the individual farmer, there are clear opportunities for suppliers to develop products or services to support them in their endeavours. The Emissions Reduction Fund that is one of the pillars of the current Australian Government's emissions reduction strategy has specific methodologies that are paying some projects for the carbon emissions they will sequester over the next decade and beyond.

Reducing food waste

Staggeringly, it has been estimated that up to half of global food production is wasted. Estimates vary and depend on many assumptions; the actual figure may be lower.[xciv] Regardless, the problem is endemic and there are many opportunities to reduce food waste at all stages of the supply chain, from the harvest to the home.

A number of issues are contractual, such as exclusive supply arrangements requiring farmers to discard produce that does not meet their customer's quality standards. Simply relaxing such conditions – which can include the sweetness of a pea, size of an apple or the bendiness of a banana – or developing alternate sales channels for differing grades of produce would immediately reduce waste and enable additional revenue.[xcv]

Contemporary distribution and communication technologies mean there are many opportunities to shorten food supply chains, reducing middlemen – to their potential detriment – but improving potential profitability for both food producers and retailers, while at the same time reducing opportunities for spoilage and waste.

Large retailers are already engaging more actively with growers and processors, and some supermarket chains have also introduced local sourcing deals, reducing logistics miles and warehousing between farm gate and individual stores.[xcvi] As well as limiting waste this tactic can also provide benefits for smaller producers and retailers who capitalise on consumers' desires to "buy local". There are many opportunities for logistics specialists and software providers to facilitate this trend.

Genetic modification and other food processing innovations may also be able to extend the shelf life of many foodstuffs, while a smart phone app linked with a supermarket's records of individuals' grocery purchases, could help consumers remember what food they have that needs eating and match the known contents of their fridge and larder with appropriate recipes. A future generation of refrigerators could track use by dates and prompt householders to either use or freeze produce before it goes off.

Sustaining seafood

Given constraints on land, it seems inevitable that we will need to extract more of our food from the oceans. However, many conventional fish stocks are already under significant pressure from over-exploitation or pollution, and are starting to be affected by ocean acidification, de-oxygenation and warming seas. Algaculture (the farming of algae or seaweed), however, offers opportunities not just for food, but also as a potential source of energy, pollution reduction (including absorption of carbon dioxide), fertiliser and bioplastic,[xcvii] plus as a habitat for other marine life.

It is likely that governments will invest in research and monitoring to ascertain the health of marine eco-systems and specific fish stocks and in turn regulate commercial fishing more tightly within their economic zonal waters. It's essential that an eco-system level view be taken so that the full impact of over fishing and by-catch can be established, given the complex series of food chains found in our oceans.

There is a major problem with the lack of control over fishing in international waters and it would not be surprising to see legal developments in this area. The issue then becomes one of enforcement – perhaps in the form of an expansion of the duties of the United Nations.

While it is easy to surmise that farmed fish is more sustainable, this is not always the case, particularly for carnivorous species such as salmon, which are typically fed wild-caught fish. Pollution of waters in and near many aquaculture operations is another growing problem.

However, there are opportunities emerging for agriculture and aquaculture businesses to combine forces: for example, protein waste from poultry operations can become fish food, while fish excrement can be used as fertiliser. There have also been developments in aquaponics systems, which combine ponds to grow fish, and then use the water from the ponds as high-nutrient water for hydroponic vegetable growing.

In fact, applying a "reduce, reuse, recycle" mantra to food production could identify many business opportunities to connect waste outputs from one part of the industry with the input requirements of other parts.

Where will we live?

Where will we live is a multi-faceted question, which covers themes such as:

- How will our cities be designed?
- What type of dwellings will we live in?
- How will they be constructed?
- What patterns of migration can we expect?

Urban design

A 2005 study found that urban areas were estimated to be expanding at a rate of 20,000 square kilometres per annum globally (an area the size of the country of Israel) as population growth and the rate of urbanisation increases the size and number of cities.[xcviii] Given many cities have evolved from what were originally rural support centres and the preferred locations for urban areas are generally on or near major water sources, 80% of this expansion is estimated to encroach upon agricultural land, putting a further squeeze on food production.

Accordingly, we need to re-think urban design to minimise suburban sprawl and create cities that are as compact and "walkable", efficient, functional, healthy and close to nature as possible.

Because cities will need to be more condensed, they will also need to be more vertical. The age of suburbs comprised of detached dwellings and generous yards, where private cars are mandatory, is in decline.

On the flip side, dense high-rise living can create issues with canyon-like over-shadowed streets, an absence of green space, poor pedestrian infrastructure and reduced neighbourly interaction. However, recent celebrated high density residential projects such as Sydney's One Central Park, with its integrated vertical gardens and helioscope (a series of mirrors directing sunlight onto the lower parts of the building and its courtyard) have demonstrated innovative approaches to overcoming such challenges.

Our future cities will need effective mass transit with prioritised or dedicated access: there's not much point building high rise apartments along existing corridors if the only transportation option remains clogged roads.

We also need to reduce distance between workers and work. In some large cities, governments are already starting to develop a network of viable sub-metropolitan employment hubs to moderate the traditional focus of the central business district and in so doing reduce travel congestion and commuting times. Teleworking and remote working, whether from a home office or a shared co-working space in one of the new satellite commercial precincts, are also growing trends as employees and managers become more accustomed to the technologies and management disciplines associated with virtual teams.

As well as good public transport (including light rail and bus-ways), sub-metropolitan hubs need to be well serviced, offering urban living, vibrant retail, entertainment and schools. It is expected that many more streets in existing and new CBDs will be largely or wholly pedestrianised around bus or light rail routes, de-emphasising use of private vehicles.

There are a number of celebrated case studies of cities that have converted urban motorway corridors to parkland and enjoyed significant social, environmental and economic benefits, such as the Cheonggyecheon Stream Restoration Project in Seoul, Korea.[xcix]

As average temperatures steadily increase, an issue of some concern is the urban heat island effect. It is caused because building mass, reduced vegetation cover and the typical use of dark colours for roofs and roadways in cities contributes to urban temperatures being up to several degrees Celsius warmer than nearby suburban and rural areas.[c]

Roof painters may also benefit as homeowners realise the indoor temperature and energy savings benefits of having their homes reflect more sunlight. Some municipalities are also experimenting with lighter coloured road surfaces,[ci] potentially providing a boon for roading contractors who can provide re-surfacing in a cost effective and efficient manner. In the big picture, energy efficiency savings due to the reduced air conditioning load associated with lower temperatures, and potentially other environmental benefits can partially offset the costs of such initiatives.

Contemporary urban planning places increased emphasis on providing green space, affording opportunities for traditional landscape gardeners and particularly those specialising in vertical and roof-top gardens. While some plants are susceptible to common urban air pollutants such as surface level ozone and sulphur dioxide[cii] others are effective at filtering a range of noxious chemicals and can be used to improve air quality, especially indoors.[ciii] This has created thriving and growing businesses for indoor plant suppliers.

Returning to the topic of localising food production, urban vegetable gardens are likely to be a growing trend, whether for personal consumption or at a commercial scale supplying restaurants, grower's markets or niche retailers.

Urban beehive businesses are also popping up, allowing users to generate honey while also providing pollination services to city growers and municipal parks. Innovations to protect both enterprises from adverse impacts of air pollution and improve crop quality may be another business opportunity.

Design and construction

While there was previously a trend in many Western countries towards larger dwelling sizes, rising energy costs and declining family sizes[15] mean that in some cases the size of new houses is starting to shrink.

For example, US construction industry data suggests that house sizes peaked in 2007 and have been trending downwards since.[civ] The timing does suggest a key influence was the onset of the global financial crisis and there are limited data points to establish the trend, however, we are also seeing growing interest in so-called micro homes and compact apartments, which can be as little as a tenth of the size of a typical suburban McMansion.

In addition to their small footprint, some micro home designs are experimenting with reused and recycled materials, with modified shipping containers a popular option. You can build or install a micro home or more conventional granny flat in the yard of many suburban homes. Various governments are also encouraging this trend and reducing the associated red tape in an effort to increase urban density and create more affordable rental housing.[cv]

Meanwhile, construction techniques are changing in three broad ways:

1. Design intended to improve thermal comfort and energy efficiency. Broadly speaking, as it gets warmer buildings will need to do a better job:[cvi]

    ▪ Keeping heat out, through effective orientation and solar design; draught-proofing and insulation;

    ▪ Soaking up inside heat using appropriate solid materials to create a heat sink (for example, rammed earth walls – an ancient technology gaining new currency); and

    ▪ Getting air moving inside the building to help occupants feel cooler, for example creating passive draughts by exploiting prevailing cool breezes with appropriately positioned windows and fans. Low speed thermostatically operated fans that circulate heat from living areas to the ceiling void during summer, and vice versa during winter can be very effective and, depending on the local climate, can replace a majority of artificial cooling and heating.

---

15   Bearing in mind that many developed nations are reproducing at less than replacement rates and there is an ever increasing number of so-called empty nester households given the ageing population.

2. Materials specification intended to reduce environmental impact. Typical structural materials such as concrete and steel are energy intensive and in the case of concrete and cement emit considerable greenhouse gases during manufacture. While use of partially recycled steel and concrete has increased, in recent years advances have also been made with engineered timber as a structural product in a growing number of mid- and high-rise buildings. Construction of a 24 level building using over 75% timber has recently been approved in Vienna, Austria, which will be one of the tallest wooden structures in the world when completed. Using timber in buildings sequesters atmospheric carbon, although it is critical that the timber is sourced from a sustainably managed forest. Depending on the circumstances timber may also convey other advantages. Advances are also being made in non-structural building materials including facades, roofing, linings, insulations, pipes, wires, paint – in fact almost every component is undergoing innovation to improve the environmental credentials and/or reduce toxicity so as to improve the health and enjoyment of the building's occupants.

3. Engineering and construction standards are being strengthened (for both residential and commercial buildings) in order to reduce damage and loss and improve occupant safety in the event of extreme weather hazards. Depending on the regional conditions this may include resilience against flooding, large hail, destructive winds, lightning strikes or bushfire protection. Even drought resilience needs to be considered: when soils dry out and the water table falls, this can lead to subsidence and other conditions affecting building foundations.[cvii] Innovations in roofing materials may improve hail resilience (including hail hardened photovoltaic panels that replace conventional roofing materials); traditional terracotta tiles and shallow roof pitches are unlikely to be favoured in hail-prone regions.

Changes in urban infrastructure and systems

Other evolving elements of urban design include our approach to energy distribution; the potential reclamation of some space that is used for vehicle parking; and a growing issue with storm water.

Traditionally electricity has been generated in large power stations located away from cities and distributed through a network of transmission lines, substations and related infrastructure. Local and neighbourhood generation schemes are challenging this model, with rooftop solar plus battery storage expected to see a growing number of homes and some types of commercial buildings go "off grid".

District schemes involving gas based co- and tri-generation plants are also necessitating changes in the way we think about designing the heating and cooling (HVAC) systems of commercial and apartment buildings: providing connection points for condenser, chilled or hot water beyond the boundary of the building and reducing the amount of HVAC equipment needed in the building itself. These changes are creating opportunities for engineering firms and in time may lead to projects to remove some centralised grid infrastructure.

We will also need more electricity infrastructure for Electric Vehicles, with parking facilities upgraded to including charging points. On the other hand, self-driving cars that can be summoned at need may help lessen the demand for parking space, particularly within congested CBDs. Parking buildings for autonomous vehicles could be provided in less expensive CBD fringe areas and could achieve significantly greater density, since it would not be necessary to provide clearances for people to access their vehicles (or the normal parking tolerances associated with human error). Curb-side parking could be repurposed for dedicated cycle-ways or vegetation.

Urban storm water infrastructure will be a massive growth industry over the next few decades as municipalities struggle to stay ahead of lawsuits from property owners and their insurers in the face of the greater frequency of extreme weather impacts.

Already the first stone has been thrown in the United States, with Farmers Insurance attracting publicity in 2014 by suing councils around greater Chicago for failing to prepare adequately for flooding that occurred in 2013 – exactly the type of extreme weather event predicted by the city's climate change adaptation plan. While Farmers later withdrew the suit, the company claimed it was sending a message encouraging municipalities to act now to prevent losses in future events.[cviii]

We're starting to see storm water provisions being expanded for new infrastructure projects. Local authorities will increasingly demand development projects incorporate high capacity storm water detention systems in order to reduce strain on the capacity of municipal drainage systems. However, with many cities' drainage infrastructure ageing, it will be necessary to dig up many roads to replace pipes. In low lying cities, as sea levels rise it will be necessary to pump storm water as pipes that have traditionally relied on gravity drainage are increasingly flooded.

Containment of sewage and its segregation from storm water will also need to be improved to reduce contamination risk. For example in Miami Beach, Florida, one of the hot spots of sea level rise, the city has recently undergone two years of modifications to an increasingly flood prone thoroughfare including resurfacing, curb and gutter modifications and the installation of drainage pumping plants.[cix]

Given the high value put on coastal property in many developed nations, there is likely to be a transitional market driven by homeowners for defenses against coastal erosion and sea level rise. Beach "renourishment" (sand replacement) and basement pumping systems may also be popular. In the United States, a market has already emerged for temporary flood barriers that are erected at the first sign of impending floods to protect exposed properties.

When it becomes impractical to defend low lying areas, enter the market for lawyers who – through class actions against local government authorities and other tactics – will seek to ensure that land owners and their insurers are at least somewhat compensated for their losses. At face value there may be a case to answer if councils and governments sit on the evidence of sea level rise and continue to support low lying development.

As well as movement away from low lying coastal property, ridgeline sites and other locations that are exposed to increasingly ferocious storms may become significantly less desirable. Suburbs may gradually be re-oriented away from destructive weather. Expansive views may no longer be considered a desirable feature given the risks they bring.

Well-heeled property owners in developed nations moving due to coastal inundation or storms are just one small facet of climate change-related migration. From low lying islands such as the Marshalls, Kiribati and the Maldives, to critically exposed nations such as Bangladesh, hundreds of millions of people will at some point be displaced by rising sea levels. Contamination of fresh water supplies and growing soils due to salt water incursion is already a major concern in such areas. In addition to individual properties, rising sea levels threaten to strand some communities or suburbs that are reached via low-lying roads, necessitating costly infrastructure investments to raise roads and facilitate storm water removal. And it's not just coastal areas that are at risk.

In various parts of the world (including developed nations such as the United States) desertification[16] has made a number of villages and small towns untenable. Populations have moved on, and once vibrant communities have become ghost towns. Author Giles Slade in his book American Exodus: Climate Change and the Coming Flight for Survival predicts a mass migration from Mexico into the United States and in turn to Canada as families gravitate towards more climatically sympathetic land.

We'll explore the sovereignty issues inherent in this prospect in a later section but for now consider the economic impact of significant resettlement. While areas with declining populations will wither, the inbound flows, particularly to developed nations that are prepared and able to accept climate immigrants will generate enormous opportunities in infrastructure, construction and supporting services businesses.

What will we buy?

As we wake up to the mountains of waste and pollution we create, it would be whimsical to think that people might decide to consume less stuff. Some will, but with a rising middle class in many parts of the world still in "catch-up" mode, there are billions of people wanting a taste of first world affluence. Globally, we're likely to remain as obsessed with brands, fashion and gadgets as ever.

However, the parameters for brand popularity may start to shift. Various surveys suggest that younger consumers are most concerned about the environment For example, a Millennial Cause Study by marketing firm Cone Communications[cx] highlighted these themes:

- 89% of Millennials (the cohort born between the 1980s and early 2000s) said they are likely or very likely to switch to a brand associated with a good cause (price and quality being equal);
- 83% said they trust a company more if it is socially/ environmentally responsible;
- 78% said they believe that companies have a responsibility to join them in this effort;

16   The process by which semi-arid and dry land ecosystems become unviable for agriculture and human settlement due to the impacts of erosion, salinity and changing weather patterns that reduce rainfall.[cxi]

- 74% said they're more likely to pay attention to a company's overall messages when that company shows a deep commitment to a cause; and

- 61% said they feel personally responsible for making a difference in the world.

As these young people begin to dominate consumer spending, we may see labels that can demonstrate less harm and more good for the environment beginning to take precedence – particularly brands with a deep and genuine sustainability story that goes beyond marketing "greenwash".

Sustainable brands

For example, Preserve is a US-based consumer products company producing items from 100% recycled plastics. It has established closed loop systems such as a toothbrush subscription service. When your brush's bristles are worn it can be returned to the company to be recycled and used to make new products. Of course, it's not quite a closed loop given the associated transportation impacts.

Or Interface, the commercial flooring company with a carpet tile leasing plan. They supply the carpet for an office fit out, maintain it during its life (replacing worn tiles in high traffic areas with replacements) and when the space needs to be refurbished, they will collect the old carpet and recycle it into new tiles using sophisticated processes that ensure almost nothing is wasted.

How about Patagonia, the outdoor-wear company that only wants you to ever buy one of their jackets? They've committed to only producing clothing designed to last the wearer's life time and have also teamed up with swap market-maker Yerdle to facilitate the transfer of previously owned items to new owners within their stores.

World-wide, brands large and small are retooling their supply chains and processes and seeking ways they can "close the loop": turning their operations into closed loop systems complete with recycling and re-use at the end of a product's life, with minimal need for fresh material inputs.

Makers of consumable products are undertaking lifecycle assessments and attempting to minimise the end-to-end impacts, changing materials and suppliers if necessary to yield lower footprint products.

In short, if your products are not genuinely responsible then they face a significant risk of become less attractive over time: initially to thinking consumers; later, by major retailers applying more discerning procurement policies; and in time by government regulation.

With this impetus, opportunities exist for organisations that can help companies improve the sustainability of their products, services, processes and operations.

They'll need partners that have efficient and environmentally friendly processes to recover, separate and recycle a growing variety of waste streams into raw materials.

For example, there will be roles for waste brokers to connect the waste of one organisation with materials demand by others (where waste cannot be re-used within the organisation itself).[17] Or for product designers whose focus is on characteristics such as durability, reusability, disassembly and recyclability in addition to functionality and aesthetics. And for those whose designs are modular and don't force consumers to buy features they just don't need. We'll need materials specialists who understand the full lifecycle implications of differing options and can advise designers on the most sustainable choices, and innovative production specialists who can take advantage of inventions such as 3D printing to produce more tightly customised products in short runs.

Examples of this trend can be seen in the development of new building materials, furniture, cleaning products and many other product categories over the last decade or two. As purchasers become more aware of their environmental choices, manufacturers that cannot claim an authentic approach to product sustainability will be sidelined by competitors that can.

Eco-labeling

To inform consumers about the environmental merits (or otherwise) of the products and services they buy, a host of service providers – including a mix of government, green groups, industry associations and private companies – have and are establishing certification schemes covering everything from fast moving consumer goods (FMCG) to computers and electronics, timber and paper, agricultural produce, seafood, clothing, furniture and buildings.

---

17   This is also part of a growing field of endeavour knows as "industrial ecology" where there is no "waste", only inputs that can be used by another manufacturer or enterprise. For example, restaurant scraps in parts of Sydney and Melbourne are being turned directly into fertiliser for agriculture via innovative on-site rapid composting units.

The better of these schemes employ comprehensive life cycle analysis (LCA, which is discussed elsewhere in this book) and chain of custody certification (which involves tracing, for example, a ream of photocopy paper back to a particular harvesting operation in a particular forest) to prove a claimed environmental benefit or reduction of harm. Others are little more than marketing tools with no basis in fact that tout the alleged advantages of a particular product to consumers, but are without metrics or evidence to support their claims.

Typically, money is made by charging companies that want to have their products certified, and such schemes (both the legitimate and the bogus ones) generally also involve setting up a network of third party individuals able to undertake the assessment process. In some cases organisations charge companies or individuals such as architects or engineers an accreditation fee and also on-going professional development fees.

The rating scheme market is highly fragmented and, in many jurisdictions and industries, poorly regulated. It is ripe for increased regulation to ensure consumers are not being misled, and consolidation or standardisation to prevent shoppers from simply being bamboozled or overwhelmed by competing organisations' claims. In developing proper controls there are also a number of contentious issues to be resolved, which will provide opportunities to the legal fraternity.

A simplified example of one such conundrum is the certification of forest products: one would like to think that timber was legally harvested (as well as being grown in a sustainable manner, though defining 'sustainable' is its own complex challenge also). If I, as a forest owner, have the necessary licenses or permits in place cut down and remove timber from my land, then is that all that is sufficient to determine the legality of the timber? What if in extracting the timber I retrospectively find I am in breach of the regulations – for example if the logging operation pollutes a nearby stream or takes a habitat tree that was marked for protection – is the timber still legally harvested? Given that by the time I become aware of the breach the timber could have been milled and dispatched to a buyer as legally harvested: if it has retrospectively deemed as illegal, how is that dealt with?

As can be seen the area of environmental certification for products and services provides plenty of scope for entrepreneurialism and maturity.

This also suggests there is also plenty of opportunity to develop a sub-industry of specialists educating consumers and advising corporate procurement departments about how to navigate the ratings and certification minefield. Indeed, at least one organisation has begun cataloguing so-called eco-labeling schemes and had over 450 on their database as of early 2015 (www. ecolabelindex.com).

In some cases it will be simple innovations that help companies thrive. In the UK, for example, a company specialising in sauces for winter meals launched a range of cold dessert sauces such as ice cream toppings. These utilised the same manufacturing and packaging technology while attracting a new and potentially growing market in the face of warmer summers and shorter winters.[cxii] In the same vein, Unilever has developed what it calls an "ice structuring protein" for frozen products that means they don't melt as quickly at above freezing temperatures, while also examining a broader range of climate change impacts and opportunities across many of its food product lines.[cxiii]

The growing personal services industry may also get a boost, particularly in more affluent areas, as households pay for other people to sort their trash in order to maximise their recycling, compost their food scraps, tend their worm farms, and service their water filters, solar and grey water systems, and so on.

Collaborative consumption

Whether driven by environmental concerns or simply a desire to get better value, the rise of collaborative consumption market places is a generally positive development. Services such as Yerdle, the in-home accommodation site Airbnb, car pooling and taxi substitutes such as Uber and Lyft, the neighbourhood share-car services GoGet and ZipCar are allowing people to profitably "share" assets such as empty rooms or share cars in a way that makes buying a car unnecessary for many people. Other initiatives such as European tool borrowing app Peerby,[cxiv] and of course eBay – the global clearing house for unwanted stuff – have made it easy for people to share, rent and responsibly dispose of resources that would typically be under utilised or sent to landfill.

From an environmental standpoint, many of these services encourage re-use or improved rates of utilisation of assets, thereby reducing embodied emissions by decreasing demand for new items. While traditional industries threatened by these market makers are fighting back, lawmakers are increasingly beginning to review archaic legislation to help usher in this new trend, albeit more often because of the benefits it brings consumers rather than because of any perceived environmental benefit.

Given the nature of the Internet, it is likely that such services will undergo a number of metamorphoses and there are likely to be opportunities for market consolidation and even more disruptive new entrants.

Another potential trend spurred in part by the rise in collaborative consumption and growing regulation, particularly in the European Union, is a shift by appliance manufacturers (or intermediaries) towards lease plans for their wares rather than outright sales. Renting white goods such as refrigerators or washing machines makes sense, particularly if you already rent your house and car. Manufacturers could provide mid-life servicing to ensure optimal energy efficiency (replacing door seals on fridges and servicing compressors, for example). Then at the appliance's end of life the provider would be obliged to ensure that its materials are recycled to the greatest possible extent.

How will we stay healthy?

The key health challenges from climate change include:

- Heat related illnesses and deaths from exposure to extreme temperatures. This will particularly impact on people who work outdoors or in non-air conditioned environments, plus infants, older people, the ill and obsese, who are more susceptible to heat stress and dehydration. Heatwaves are already a leading cause of death compared to other types of natural disasters (particularly in developed nations where preparedness levels for violent storms and earthquakes generally lead to significantly fewer fatalities than those affecting developing nations). For example, excess mortality[18] of up to 70,000 people was associated with the severe European heatwave of 2003.[cxv] Higher temperatures may also provide excuses for some people to exercise less, potentially increasing rates of health conditions associated with a more sedentary lifestyle.

---

18   Excess mortality measures the difference between actual and typical death rates expected in a given area for a given time of the year.

- Water supply contamination during extreme precipitation and flood events. Flooding in Brisbane, Australia in 2011 led to the temporary closure of one of the main water treatment plants as the incoming water was too muddy to be treated. On that occasion water supply interruptions were avoided on that occasion by re-routing supply from other treatment plants and implementing demand reduction strategies.[cxvi] However, there are likely to be increasing situations where extreme weather jeopardises fresh water supplies or people are otherwise forced to drink untreated water, potentially leading to a range of health issues.

- A related issue is more direct exposure to flood waters and the after-effect of floods. It is not uncommon in many areas for sewage systems to overflow during significant flooding, raising infection rates. Receding flood waters can become breeding grounds for mosquitos and other potentially harmful insects. Mould in buildings resulting from exposure to flood waters can in turn cause a variety of health conditions. And of course the murky and often fast moving water presents public safety issues for people unfortunate or unwary enough to find themselves trapped or engulfed. Drownings are frequent.

- More generally, a rise in the frequency and/or intensity of extreme weather events may result in greater injuries / illnesses and demand for emergency services.

- The spread of tropical, insect-borne diseases to areas in higher altitudes and higher latitudes as it becomes warmer. Insect carriers of such diseases thrive in the tropics because it is warm overnight and all year round, meaning no die off in cooler months as is common in temperate climates. Meteorologists are already observing milder winters and warmer nights in many areas as the atmosphere retains more heat.[cxvii]

- Additional health risks arise from the greater expected incidence of bush fires (not to mention an increase in lightning strikes). For example, during the summer of 2010 an estimated 55,000 people died in Russia from a combination of a severe heat wave and smoke inhalation from a resultant series of major bush fires.[cxviii] Respiratory ailments such as asthma are likely to be exacerbated by bushfires and other climatic changes. Allergen patterns may also change.

Moving forward – opportunities in health

Given these challenges (and coupled with ageing populations and a rise in non-communicable diseases in many countries, both of which are potentially further exacerbated by the impacts of climate change), the healthcare and safety sector is growing and opportunities abound.

For starters there is likely to be increasing demand for health professionals and emergency workers, requiring growth in the associated infrastructure, hospital beds and education. Hospitals located in regions exposed to extreme weather will need to be made more resilient, providing construction and engineering opportunities.

Given concerns with disease transmission, medical facilities produce a great deal of waste. A wide range of equipment is now provided as single use sterile consumables, for example the tubing and needles used for insulin pumps. Recycling rates for medical waste (and its packaging) are relatively low and there is potential opportunity for niche providers to build markets, though the value of the recyclable materials may not always deliver a positive business case unless the process can be subsidised by the producer of the waste or incorporated in a higher purchase price.

Alternatively, new technologies may be found to change the way common medical procedures are carried out in order to reduce the waste, for example, the nanopatch vaccines under development in Australia, which do away with syringes altogether.

The increasing frequency of very hot days means it will no longer be economically feasible to shut down construction sites or other outdoor-work zones or close non-air conditioned schools and factories on very hot days. Adaptations may include employee monitoring devices that sense body temperature or signs of dehydration and warn supervisors so that individuals can be given breaks.[19] Staff will require training in prevention and spotting the warning signs of heat stress. In some hot climates companies are already pioneering personal protective equipment (PPE) for construction and factory

---

19 Incidentally, as of early 2015 unobtrusive body temperature and hydration sensors have not yet been successfully incorporated into the growing number of "iGadgets" such as Fitbits and the Apple iWatch. Body temperature requires a reading within the body's "core" (such as in the mouth or under the armpit): temperatures at extremities such as the wrist need to be adjusted for ambient temperature. Currently there is no reliable test for hydration apart from one involving use of a specimen jar. With the growing interest in health monitoring gadgets, however, there is plenty of scope for researchers to crack that challenge.[cx]

workers, such as ventilated hard hats (perhaps with the addition of solar powered fans) and reflective vests with built in frozen gel packs to help keep workers cool. Portable solar powered refrigeration to keep employees' drinks cool may also grow market share beyond their current camping and fishing applications.

Much as it would be nice to think that passive ventilation systems will suffice, manufacturers of air conditioning systems are sure to benefit – particularly those that deliver breakthroughs in energy efficiency and/or pioneer new refrigerants that are not also potent greenhouse gases (to replace the current hydro fluorocarbon or HFC based technologies).

There will be roles for emergency response specialists in establishing plans to activate heat-wave shelters across major cities, utilising convention centres, indoor sports arenas and other large air conditioned spaces. These will also need to be equipped with standby generators or battery storage, as heat waves are often accompanied by utility power supply interruptions due to the extreme load from everyone turning on their cooling, as was seen in January 2014 in Melbourne.[cxix]

Personal water purification systems are likely to become more popular, including both those that are connected to utility fresh water supplies, and field systems that can be used when utility supplies fail with whatever water sources happen to be available. In coastal communities, particularly in developing nations, personal desalination kits may provide part of the solution.

Advances in managing industrial emissions that are aimed at improving air quality in the developing world may be partially negated by increased pollution from bush fires. There is likely to be a ready market for face masks and air filtration systems for the foreseeable future in addition to treatments for people suffering from respiratory conditions triggered by bad air (which may be exacerbated by increasing temperatures). Various nascent initiatives are underway to use big data to track and predict health impacts associated with climate change.[cxxi]

Just as indoor football and cricket arenas filled a niche for people wanting to play their sport in inclement weather, increasing heat may push a broader range of sports indoors, further fuelling construction and air conditioning opportunities. Coaches and personal trainers specialising in hot weather training for athletes will be in demand, providing opportunities for specialists from tropical areas as the heat spreads pole-wards.[cxxii]

Oxitec is one company that hopes to profit from the spread of tropical disease vectors. The UK-based biotechnology firm was (as at the time of writing) seeking US Food and Drug Administration (FDA) approval to release millions of genetically modified mosquitos in a small community in the Florida Keys[cxxiii] to test their effectiveness in sterilising the resident mosquito population – which has been causing dengue fever outbreaks – by mating with them. This follows prior and promising trials in developing nations such as Brazil. Other more mundane companies that may benefit as disease-carrying mosquitos or other insects move into major population centres in developed nations are the makers of insecticides, personal repellents and insect screens.

How will we protect and defend ourselves?

There have been several papers published analysing the so-called Arab Spring uprisings, which commenced in late 2010 and led to the replacement of a number of long-term regimes in Tunisia, Egypt, Libya and Yemen.[cxxiv] It has been argued that climatic impacts, including heat waves and droughts affecting several major grain exporting countries, caused food prices to increase significantly. While not attempting to make a direct link between climate change and these mass outbreaks of civil unrest, the reduced food supply and consequent spike in prices – in countries where food accounts for a significant proportion of consumer spending – suggests that climatic variability may have been one of a number of stressors or catalysts.

It is possible to imagine a future in which food riots (such as have already occurred in dozens of countries this century), water riots and other climate related unrest becomes commonplace, potentially providing opportunities for suppliers to police, military and related civil defense forces.

Climate migration

The impacts of climate change are generally expected to be more acutely felt in the countries that are least equipped to adapt due to a lack of financial resources or stable government. Many families and communities are likely to be displaced for a variety of reasons, potentially including:

- Declining agricultural output due to drought / desertification or the inability of traditional crops to adapt to warmer temperatures.

- Communities based on flood plains where the frequency of destructive floods is increasing.

- Reduced rainfall patterns or glacial / snow pack retreat curtailing seasonal melt-water flows, in turn leading to marginalisation of fresh water supplies and/or encroaching desertification.

- Coastal communities faced with rising sea levels, particularly in conjunction with more frequent and severe storm surges. Even in wealthy countries there will come a time when it is more practical to abandon seaside villages and towns rather than rebuilding them.

- Communities threatened by bush fires.

- Civil unrest associated with the symptoms above.

It is anticipated that many millions of people will become so-called "climate migrants" in the coming decades, moving both locally and internationally in an exodus the likes of which hasn't been seen since the end of the last world war. As such, governments and municipalities in less (or beneficially) affected areas need to be preparing plans to deal with this potential population influx. There are legal questions to be answered, and also housing, schools, social services and supporting infrastructure will need to be provided in cities or countries receiving such migrants.

There is also likely to be an associated investment in border control systems to reduce the level of illegal climate migration, benefitting a range of suppliers to the relevant government agencies.

Defence challenges

Climate change presents other defense-related opportunities, including markets for products and services related to natural disaster preparation and response and the greater potential for armed conflict if seriously affected nations seek to appropriate their neighbours' water, food, energy and other natural assets by force.

In fact, a think tank known as the Global Military Advisory Council on Climate Change (GMACCC) has been established to provide guidance to military forces on climate change preparedness. National defense forces have published a variety of position papers, such as the United States' Department of Defense's Climate Change Adaptation Roadmap.[cxxv]

Given the displays of increasingly sophisticated military capability by China and other exposed nations, regional conflict is a real possibility, benefitting a range of defense-dependent industries supplying the armed forces. China, for example, is grappling with a "perfect storm" of water supply and management issues as it struggles to provide its 1.4 billion inhabitants and massive manufacturing industry with sufficient fresh water (and water-intensive food and energy) amidst rapidly declining aquifers, decadal reduction in Himalayan snow/ice melt affecting major river systems, and years of pollution compromising the quality of water courses.[cxxvi]

At a more localised level, the need for surveillance and protection of forests, marine reserves and other such assets from illegal logging and poaching will become more acute.

When US President Obama announced a significant expansion of the Pacific Remote Islands National Marine Monument in mid-2014,[cxxvii] making it off limits to commercial fishing, he increased it by nearly 800,000 square kilometres (an area about the size of Turkey or Pakistan). Monitoring an area of this size for illicit activity when government resources for such surveillance and enforcement are already stretched, means there may be increased opportunities for the private sector to offer solutions in this space. For example, satellite imagery and "big data" analytics could be used to identify and predict the movement of illicit fishing vessels so that coast guard patrols can be more effectively deployed.

It's also possible that some governments will tighten restrictions on foreign ownership of agricultural and water rights assets to ensure future food and water security. For example, understanding their domestic constraints, the Chinese have been active in snapping up major food supply assets in other countries, including Australia and southern Africa. In some cases they have made major investments in roads, railways and ports in such countries in order to provide modern infrastructure to get their wares back to Chinese consumers.[cxxviii]

Responding to disasters

Turning to the growing incidence of natural disasters, the supply of sand-bags is just the beginning. Given the breadth of issues, from hurricane-force winds and tornados to hail, bush fires, heat waves, flooding and even increased lightning strikes, there are a multitude of opportunities for companies to develop or innovate products and services to assist with disaster prevention, response and recovery.

One such example is AEERIS, a commercially operated early warning network service, which aggregates emergency data from multiple government sources (such as the Bureau of Meteorology, State Emergency Services, Rural Fire Services, Police and so on) and provides customised alerts and updates to help people make timely informed decisions about protecting their property and themselves.

Another is a fire retardant gel that can be sprayed onto homes ahead of a forest fire, significantly reducing the combustibility of the building and minimising losses. After the fire the gel is simply hosed off with water.

In terms of forest fire prevention, a current hot topic involves upgrades to spark arrestor technologies for electricity transmission lines and the associated clearing of surrounding vegetation to minimise fire ignition risk. Some utilities are scrambling to upgrade ageing infrastructure after sustaining multi-million dollar damages claims after their infrastructure was found to be responsible for sparking the tragic and destructive Black Saturday bushfires in Victoria, Australia in 2009.[cxxix]

In recent years some communities have been faced with repeated flooding, resulting in costly clean ups, heart breaking loss of family heirlooms, longer-term damage to homes, and occasional injury or death. Short of leaving the area, residents may be open to products or services that will reduce their future risks. From simple things like water and/or fire proof filing cabinets for key family documents, to water proofing or flood barrier technologies to prevent the incursion of flood waters into homes, there are likely to be many opportunities in this space if pricing models can be made attractive to consumers. As we saw earlier, expanded storm water drains, raised roads, pumping systems and controls to minimize the risks of floodwaters becoming contaminated with sewage services are also critical.

What will we do?

The foregoing sections have outlined a range of potential new jobs arising as a result of a changing climate. There are plenty of other possibilities, many of which have not yet been thought of. For example, who would have dreamed even a decade or two ago that people would be making sometimes enormous amounts of money posting YouTube videos of themselves playing and commentating on computer games? If the early 2000s has been about digital disruption and adaptation of traditional business models to the Internet, the next few decades are going to see a raft of new roles relating to the mitigation of and adaptation to climate change and other environmental issues.

So far we've seen new roles such as Energy Efficiency Managers, Chief Sustainability Officers and Climate Treaty Negotiators. Demand for Climatologists (the atmospheric scientists who study and predict long term climate trends) and related specialists who can predict local impacts such as sea level, temperature and acidity; agricultural suitability; implications for construction; and so on, may increase as companies and governments seek to understand trends affecting their particular assets and regions.

Meanwhile the philanthropic Rockefeller Foundation has begun handing out grants to fund the new position of a Chief Resilience Officer in a number of major global cities, reflecting the need for municipalities (and companies) to prepare to avoid the worst impacts of climate change.[cxxx] In the financial markets, ESG[20] Analysts are a new breed of researcher who assess the environmental and social governance attributes and track record of subject companies and governments in order to inform investment decisions. Not to mention Carbon Traders, who provide liquidity to markets for carbon credits.

There are dozens of publications and conferences that have launched in recent years to spread information about sustainability and climate change, making "green" journalism and communication a viable career path.

Transformation of work

Another facet to the question "what will we do?" is, "how will we work?"

We've seen the decline of traditional manufacturing roles in developed nations and the development of services based economies, a trend that will continue as the making of things is increasingly automated.

In many services organisations, a trend towards distributed working is gaining pace, with many organisations containing virtual teams made up

20   ESG – Environmental, Social and Governance, often used interchangeably with CSR – Corporate Social Responsibility

of members in different cities and countries, who seldom if ever meet each other face to face. Increasingly, virtual teams are formed across organisational boundaries, and include a mix of direct employees, contractors, consultants and service providers.

Video conferencing and immersive collaboration technologies are becoming more pervasive within major corporations, spurred by their success on consumer devices such as smart phones and by advances in network security and bandwidth. The concept that work should be something you do, rather than somewhere you go is taking root.

However, fewer people are working from home than the technology would seem to allow. Many people still commute to CBD-based office buildings and work pretty standardised hours, a habit that contributes to traffic congestion, high transport emissions and massive loss of productive time in transit.

The reasons for this apparent inefficiency are varied but include factors such as:

- Out-moded management styles, which value "presenteeism" as opposed to outputs and outcomes.

- A belief that corporate culture and innovation goals can be enhanced when people are co-located and can benefit from casual and serendipitous encounters. Technology giants Google and Yahoo have recently made policy announcements discouraging remote work.[cxxxi]

- Concerns regarding the security of corporate data.

- Perhaps more compellingly, the fact that humans are gregarious creatures, and thrive on social interaction. Traditionally this has been difficult to achieve from the solitude of a home office, given lower tolerance for the use of telephony and electronic media as a social communications tool when used in a workplace setting.

In recent years there has been an explosion in co-working sites, which can be rented casually or formally by individuals and corporations. Many of these are opening in satellite city and suburban locations, providing opportunities for people to enjoy a level of social interaction (albeit with people who may not work for the same organisation), a structured workplace setting that affords fewer personal distractions than may be the case working from home, and, from an Adaptive Economy point of view, the opportunity to significantly reduce commuting distances and associated emissions.

The bottom line is, given availability of the right technology and appropriate management attitudes there are relatively few office-based roles that cannot be accomplished from co-working sites.

Meanwhile in the office, the traditional idea of each employee having their own desk has been challenged by the advent of so-called "activity based working" which is often dumbed down to a desk sharing arrangement that recognises that office occupancy levels are typically no greater than 60% on any given day (due to illness, vacation, meetings and business travel).

Organisations adopting such arrangements have typically reported real estate savings of around 20% along with associated energy savings, meaning less growth pressure on urban office space. High rates of adoption create an environmental win and potentially allow older office building stock to be redeveloped as apartments as part of the urban transformation discussed earlier.

A further advantage of unassigned office seating arrangements include the fact that the fitout doesn't need to be modified every time teams change membership or the organization restructures, leading to a potentially significant reduction in construction and demolition waste.

On the flip-side, activity-based working does not suit every worker, nor is it suitable for every role. This is where specialists in workforce psychology, workspace planning and the spatial dimensions of human resources will find opportunities to ensure a nuanced response that is productive for key workers and still ensures the organization has a lean and environmentally conscious office footprint.

Chapter 6
Reversal of Misfortune

A recent, peer reviewed article in the journal Science by a global scientific team under the auspices of the Stockholm Resilience Centre (SRC)[cxxxii] considers a number of "planetary boundaries" relating to the "safe operating space for humanity based on the intrinsic biophysical processes that regulate the stability of the Earth System".

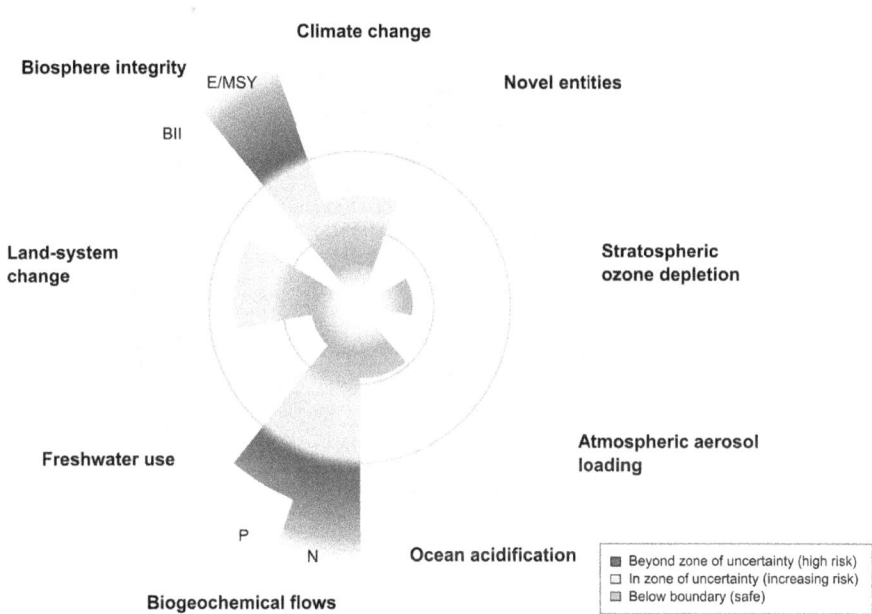

Figure 9 – Planetary boundaries summary (used with permission)

The authors contend that if these boundary limits are significantly exceeded for extended periods of time, then we are putting our society and way of life at risk. While the planet has experienced and bounced back from periods where one or more of these boundaries has been broken (such as the asteroid impact that is thought to have wiped out the dinosaurs about 65 million years ago), humanity's time scale is incredibly short compared to the multi-millennial duration it might take to recover from some of the environmental havoc we are currently wreaking. Figure 9 and Table 2 summarise the SRC findings.

Status	Boundary	Description
Boundary significantly exceeded (high risk)	Biosphere integrity	Species extinction and loss of biodiversity
	Biogeochemical flows	Use of nitrogen and phosphorus based fertilisers and associated runoff into waterways and oceans
Boundary exceeded (increasing risk)	Climate change	Build up of anthropogenic greenhouse gases in the atmosphere
	Land system change	The level of remaining forest cover
Boundary at risk of being exceeded	Ocean acidification	Increasing acidification of oceans due to dissolved carbon dioxide associated with anthropogenic greenhouse gases
Boundary not exceeded (low risk)	Freshwater use	Availability of fresh water for human and environmental uses
	Stratospheric ozone depletion	Level of exposure to harmful solar UV radiation. This has been controlled due to the impact of the Montreal Protocol
New boundary, not yet quantified	Chemical pollution and the release of novel entities	Emissions of pollutants such as synthetic organic compounds (including plastics), heavy metals, and radioactive waste
	Atmospheric aerosol loading	Anthropogenic emissions of aerosols such as smoke and dust, which can have a variety of climatic and health impacts

Table 2 – Planetary boundaries summary

With the breadth and extent of these problems becoming ever more apparent, public funding and private philanthropy as well as commercial demand is driving the emergence of new technologies and services that can help clean up the mess. In Pixar's endearing film Wall-E we were treated to a dystopian future where humanity had abandoned a planet that it had made uninhabitable: water starved, soils eroded, subject to destructive dust storms, covered in litter and devoid of natural life. The titular character in the film is a small robot whose role is to collect and compact cubes of trash and build it into sky-scraper high stacks while the remains of humanity await the restoration of a habitable planet in resort-style space ships. This is, of course, exactly the kind of idea we want to stay in the realms of fiction.

But there's a take away – rather than simply stacking trash ever higher, a better idea is to improve efforts to collect, sort, recycle and reprocess as much waste as possible. For example, over recent years attention has been focused on the Pacific Gyre and other massive ocean waste dumps of floating plastic. Recent research estimated that around eight million tonnes of plastic waste makes its way into the oceans each year. Collectively there are trillions of bits of plastic, the oils in which attract and concentrate toxic dioxins, which are gradually poisoning the marine ecosystem and the seafood we consume as they are ingested.[cxxxiii] While efforts to date have been trivial, a number of companies such as Method and Bionic Yarn are marketing products – from traditional plastic products to faux denim jeans – made from recovered ocean plastic.

On land, projects to remediate humankind's environmental damage and restore productive ecosystems will produce many opportunities. Waste and recycling services are already global businesses, with the likes of Suez Environment and Veolia investing in increasingly sophisticated waste sorting and recycling technologies. One such innovation is a machine for processing waste printed circuit boards (PCBs) from computers, TVs, phones and so on, back to their component materials. PCBs are first shredded into dust, which is then passed through an alkali bath to separate the various elements including gold, mercury, rare earths and so on.[cxxxiv]

Before we think about recycling, though, there is a lot more work that can be done to reduce unnecessary production. Food waste, covered in a previous chapter, is only one facet. There is a considerable amount of over-production and pre-consumer waste generated by many consumer durables. On a tour of an eWaste specialist's operation, for example, I was horrified to see workers disassembling and crushing brand new unsold LED TVs (complete with their original packaging).

The reasons I was given for this waste of resources were:

1. Some were slightly damaged items where economics dictated that it was more cost effective for the manufacturer to claim on its insurance and dispose of the item than to off-load it to a seconds outlet; and,

2. Some were remaindered stock of discontinued models.

Pre-consumer eWaste accounted for 15% of that recycler's volume.

The SRC's Planetary Boundaries paper echoes many studies that have called out the deleterious effects of Nitrogen and Phosphorous-based fertilisers, pesticides, sediment and other agricultural runoff into waterways (and eventually oceans).

There, such chemicals inhibit the normal ecosystems, limiting aquatic life while promoting the build-up of algae and other pests including toxic blooms and the destructive crown of thorns starfish. There are enormous opportunities for producers of cost effective products and services that can be implemented by farmers (potentially with government assistance) to reduce this pollution. Various government agencies including the NSW Department of Water Resources[cxxxv] have published guidelines that can assist with better management practices such as:

- Improving fencing to keep livestock away from streams
- Planting and maintaining healthy vegetation around streams
- Creating or restoring coastal wetland systems
- Building retention ponds to capture and re-use runoff
- Recycling systems for greenhouse wastewater
- Covers or enclosures for fertiliser and manure storage
- Sealing dirt roads
- Systems to help growers better target and therefore reduce fertiliser and pesticide use
- Upgrading to more efficient irrigation systems
- Mechanically aerating compacted soils to increase infiltration and reduce runoff
- Development of oyster or other shellfish beds to filter nutrient-rich coastal waters, while also providing a saleable food source
- Establishment of pollution rights and trading schemes, which transfer costs back to polluters

Another opportunity for coastal rehabilitation involves the use of algaculture, which as we saw earlier could become an important foodstuff, while also sequestering carbon dioxide.

Wherever you look there are other examples of environmental degradation that may provide opportunities for innovative organisations either specialising in rehabilitation or using rehabilitation projects as a catalyst for other commercial endeavours.

For example, in Australia alone there are estimated to be over 50,000 abandoned mine sites[cxxxvi] and the scarred landscape of some parts of the continent make it look like a Swiss cheese from the air. Many of these sites are unsightly, dangerous, and continue to pollute the local environment and water supply with dangerous chemicals long after mining activity has ceased. The Post Mining Alliance has produced the book *101 Things to do with a Hole in the Ground* that includes real remediation projects to provide inspiration for those faced with the clean up task.

Unfortunately, given lax environmental standards, in many cases mine remediation will rely on taxpayer funding, so projects that generate income to cover at least part of the costs (including secondary mining, industrial, tourism, recreational, and other uses) will be particularly attractive.[cxxxvii]

There are thought to be around 8.7 million species of living things (plants and animals) on earth.[cxxxviii] While species become extinct naturally – often when they outgrow their food supply – the current extinction rate, at 100 per million species per year (one in 10,000), is estimated to be 1,000 times faster than the natural rate of about 1 species per decade[cxxxix] and at least 10 times above what the SRC study posits as a safe threshold. While it's easy to dismiss the loss of creatures such as the Cape Verde giant skink (in 2013) or the Hainan ormosia (a type of legume, in 1997), the truth is that in many cases scientists don't fully understand the importance of particular species within their eco-systems and food chains.

Of current cause for great concern is the widespread failure of bee populations. Not only are bees a source of nutritious honey, they also provide a critical pollination service for both wild plants and many farm-grown crops. Whole hives are literally collapsing – and it is currently not clear why – and the phenomenon has affected up to 50% of colonies in some countries. Theories include the effects of prolonged exposure to agricultural and domestic pesticides, loss of habitat and associated malnutrition. Whatever the causes, the effects are rising prices for both honey and also for pollination services for farmers. At risk is an estimated $200 billion annually of critical food crops.

Meanwhile, research from the University of Michigan has confirmed that the neurotoxin mercury has been polluted from industrial sites in such quantities that it has dispersed globally and led to an appreciable increase in concentrations in the open ocean. Wild ocean fish species such as tuna are now being found with mercury levels bordering on unsafe according to the United States Environmental Protection Agency's scale.[cxl]

Clearly, more research is needed urgently to understand these types of phenomena and gain a deeper appreciation of how our ecosystems actually work. Organisations that can identify, protect and enhance the critical natural vectors that underpin our food supply and the health of forests and marine eco systems are likely to do well as more value and investment is placed on protecting our natural capital.

The information technology industry can help by developing more sophisticated and affordable systems for mapping, tracking and analysing the various forms of environmental degradation and depletion, including tracking species decline. Again, the use of big data and analytic tools may yield insights that can help with remediation and reversal.

Another avenue for research and development will include improving our understanding of the SRC's so-called "novel entities" including how they react in nature over the short, medium and longer term. As substances are found to be deleterious (and are legislated against), there will be opportunities to help firms re-engineer industrial processes to reduce their use; prevent them from escaping into the atmosphere, water or soils; and/or to introduce less harmful substitutes. Similarly, technologies to trap more aerosols such as carbon soot before they escape into the atmosphere will be popular, particularly in countries grappling with chronic air pollution such as China and India.

Geo-engineering

Responses to the planetary boundary of climate change have partially been covered in earlier chapters, in terms of mitigation or reduction of anthropogenic greenhouse gas emissions. But there is another potential approach that is gaining traction – the concept of geo-engineering: the direct manipulation of the earth's climate system.

There are two broad approaches to geo-engineering: one involves the development of technologies to remove carbon dioxide or other warming gases from the atmosphere and so assist the earth in returning to previous equilibrium levels, which should arrest the warming trend. The other, known as solar radiation management (SRM), involves introducing a cooling force on the climate system to counteract the warming force of greenhouse gases.[cxli]

There are a variety of approaches towards removing carbon dioxide from the atmosphere, one of the most straight-forward and potentially environmentally beneficial being re-forestation, that is, planting trees. This approach also addresses another of the SRC's boundaries, and would deliver opportunities for land owners, forestry specialists, ecologists and other disciplines. Recreational uses would follow.

Emerging carbon dioxide removal technologies include BECCS (bio-energy, carbon capture and storage). This approach takes biomass (plants) to extract carbon dioxide through photosynthesis and then burns them for energy production, capturing and sequestering the atmospheric carbon using similar storage technologies proposed for carbon dioxide extracted at source from, for example, coal fired power stations. Scrubbing towers and so-called artificial trees that use chemical processes to extract atmospheric carbon and convert it to a non-volatile solid form are also being investigated.

For entrepreneurs, the lure of widespread emissions trading schemes, which would allow them to generate and sell certificates for sequestered greenhouse gases to emitting companies is driving research into these technologies. There is still a lot of work to do to prove the efficacy of many such schemes, demonstrate that they do not involve environmentally harmful side effects, and deliver benefits cost effectively at scale.

SRM on the other hand, doesn't actually fix the root cause of warming and instead introduces a new anthropogenic impact on the climate, with unpredictable and geographically variable results. One concept that was popularised some years ago by celebrity economists Steven Levitt and Stephen Dubner in their book Superfreakonomics is to simulate the cooling effect of a major volcano by firing sulphur dioxide into the stratosphere (the upper part of the atmosphere that begins about 10km above sea level) via lightweight tubes held aloft by a series of balloons.

Another idea is to launch a massive array of mirrors into orbit some distance from earth, which would be used to deflect some of the sun's rays, thereby cooling the planet (or at least parts of it). Having ignorantly altered earth's climate system with devastating consequences through our greenhouse gas emissions, it seems like significant hubris to think that humans could attempt to fix the problem by dabbling with such complex and still relatively poorly understood mechanisms without a high risk of adverse side effects. Nevertheless, there are venture capitalists willing to invest in such plans.

More terrestrial scale projects include the lighter coloured roofs and road surfaces discussed earlier, which improve heat reflectivity and help to arrest the urban heat island effect. There is even a novel concept involving micro-bubbles and commercial shipping. In the latter, ships' propellers would be modified (using existing technologies) so that the bubbles produced from the churning motion would be significantly reduced in size. This both reduces friction as the boat moves through the water (reducing energy consumption) and creates white wakes that could last up to a day instead of dissipating rapidly as they do today. These reflective wakes, multiplied by the tens of thousands of commercial vessels, could, it is thought, provide up to a 0.5 degree reduction in global average temperatures by reducing the absorption of heat by the oceans.[cxlii]

Another growing planetary threat is ocean acidification, which is a by-product of climate change. Turning down the heat through geo engineering only solves part of the problem if we continue to change the chemical composition of the oceans to the point that marine eco-systems suffer massive collapses (when corals and krill can no longer form protective calcium carbonate shells, or due to the associated reduction in the oxygen content of the water).

Naturally the geo engineering adherents have a potential solution for this, which would involve mining and distributing mineral dust into the seas via a large fleet of ships.[cxliii] This could be a good replacement for assets stranded as the coal industry tails off, but again considerable research would be necessary to understand the second and third order consequences of such a strategy.

Chapter 7
Steady State Sustainability

In a similar vein to the Planetary Boundaries research introduced in the previous chapter, various researchers have attempted to calculate the burden our current population and way of life places on our planet's ability to support us, using measures of our environmental impact known as ecological footprints.

It is estimated that we exceeded the carrying capacity of Earth around 45 years ago, and that our current rate of consumption and pollution would require the resources of at least 1.5 Earths to be sustainable in the long run. Another way of looking at it is that it takes the planet 18 months "to regenerate what we use in a year".[cxliv] Apparently, if all seven billion of us simultaneously adopted the way of life of people in the United States, we would need up to five Earths. Clearly, with population and income levels generally rising, something eventually needs to give.

Our economy and the environment are inextricably linked, but we currently do not have effective accounting mechanisms to cost and value our use of the environment. For example, flat screen TVs are fairly cheap these days, but if you trace and value the environmental impact up the supply chain back to the raw materials, plus the consumer's lifecycle use and eventual disposal of it, the actual costs may be many times the purchase price.

These hidden costs are referred to by economists as externalities, and in the case of the TV they include the exploitation of finite resources, the pollution and greenhouse gas emissions associated with the production and transportation of the TV, the loss of any beneficial environmental value of the land used for the factory (perhaps it was constructed on a drained wetland), the non-recyclability of parts of the TV and its packaging materials.

A typical example of an externality is a factory that doesn't get charged for pumping effluent waste into a nearby stream. The costs of cleaning up the stream become a burden to society at large, and, if they are dealt with at all, are eventually paid for by taxpayers. Effectively, the firm has benefited from a free service and this has enabled them to produce goods and then sell them at a lower cost.

Take a country like New Zealand, whose economy in recent years has benefitted from the export of dairy products, largely to China. However, dairy farming is land intensive (and some farmers have been cutting down bush land to convert it to pasture), requires chemical fertilizer and weed killers (which pollute watercourses and affects the balance of coastal marine life), consumes a lot of water, and produces considerable methane emissions (which as we have seen are contributing to global warming and climate change). None of these externalities are charged to the farmer or reflected in the cost of milk, butter or cheese.

A recent study by Massey University researchers[cxlv] has estimated that the environmental impacts of the dairy industry, if converted to dollar values, could in fact exceed the export receipts (about NZD$11 billion per annum) associated with the dairy industry.

The problem of abandoned mine sites raised in the previous chapter represents another externality. Obliging miners to remediate the mess and pollution they create may in some cases have made mining projects uneconomically viable by adding additional costs.

The "small government", free market policies favoured by many politicians ignores the advice of many eminent economists that market mechanisms repeatedly fail to effectively price such externalities, therefore transferring the burden of a degraded environment either to tax payers or future generations.

Many governments have focused on increasing Gross Domestic Product (GDP). But GDP was never intended to be the proxy for the health of a nation it has become, and is in fact a narrow and perverse measure of economic progress.

For example, if I clear fell a forest and sell the timber in one year, then the proceeds from the sale of timber count towards GDP. But then I have future costs associated with rehabilitation, replanting and no income for at least 25 years: this is not anywhere reflected in GDP measures, except perhaps the labour and materials associated with replanting. As an accounting framework, GDP simply does not measure the sustainability of economic activity.

Another example is the work funded by insurers, the government and private individuals to clean up and rebuild after floods. It counts towards GDP, which illogically means a country can inflate its GDP by having lots of natural disasters. How is that considered progress?

Chasing GDP growth also promotes population growth. It's mankind's runaway population growth that, to a large extent, has created our environmental pickle. We are so numerous, our impact on the planet is enormous, and there is a level of hubris inherent in the view that we can keep expanding without reaching a limit on resources.

And there is also increasing evidence that the pursuit of economic and material growth does not actually improve happiness or quality of life, with some developed economies reporting declining levels of happiness despite what might be considered reasonable levels of growth.

Part of the problem seems to be that increasing growth and the wealth that flows from it has tended to magnify income inequality, with vast differences between the levels of wealth of even average people when compared to the top few percent.

In fact the conventional wisdom that a strong economy is necessary to create a higher quality of life is being turned on its head. A number of examples are now demonstrating that putting the focus on quality of life improves the attractiveness of a city or country to immigrants, which then spurs economic growth.[21]

Several governments have made progress towards creating a more broad reaching measure of a nation's progress, which takes into account the future well being of its peoples.

A growing number of companies are also adopting so-called "triple bottom line" accounting principles, which attempt to value not only the financial impact of the company's activities, but also its societal and environmental impacts. Generally however, appropriate valuation of environmental externalities or use of natural capital is still a long way off.

Our current systems of democratic government seem fundamentally flawed in their promotion of a narrow focus on unsustainable short-term growth. And increasingly, Western governments are influenced to an unhealthy extent by major corporations, whose agendas are similarly driven by their objective

21   Adapted from a speech given by Tim Williams, Chief Executive, Committee for Sydney, 23/4/15

to maximize shareholder returns in the short-term, a theme we'll return to later in the book.

Although the Chinese totalitarian system is far from perfect, it does have the advantage of a long term focus. As much in response to the fact that its citizens are keeling over from soot and other industrial pollution as due to the challenge of global warming and climate change, China has recently committed to stabilising its emissions from the burning of coal and peaking its greenhouse gas emissions by 2030.[cxlvi] This is a significant commitment given its starting point compared to low-growth, developed nations.

Is there an alternative path that charts a course between today's extreme political ideologies and offers a workable solution? Economic think tank the Centre for the Advancement of the Steady State Economy (CASSE) has produced a plausible manifesto in its book Enough is Enough.

It envisages an economy designed so that growth is no longer mandatory, which would be managed using a balanced scorecard of measures that takes into account "sustainable scale, fair distribution of wealth, efficient allocation of resources, and high quality of life" using a combination of market and regulatory mechanisms within a democratic framework.

CASSE does not promote communism or a tightly centrally managed economy, but seeks to shift the measurement focus to concentrate on indicators that really matter to people and the environment beyond today's narrow focus on GDP. However, it does suggest some regulatory intervention would be necessary to limit income inequality including a minimum livable wage and a cap on maximum incomes. The latter would be a difficult sell in many societies where the right of the individual to profit from his or her success is considered inviolable. It also promotes a general reduction in working hours to enable greater leisure time along with reduced production and self-gratifying consumption of "stuff".

What would CASSE's proposal mean in terms of business opportunities for a steady state economy? Many of the mitigation, adaptive and environmental regenerative opportunities outlined in earlier chapters are broadly compatible, although the nature of the corporate structure may change. For example, CASSE expects growth in the number of cooperative businesses, which are democratically owned and operated by their employees. Other enterprises that could thrive include:

- Services based businesses that help improve quality of life or provide high quality leisure experiences, particularly those that improve social interaction.
- Education services, particularly for disadvantaged groups and developing countries.
- Small scale, localised agriculture and associated markets.
- Localised micro-finance providers who can help provide capital for community projects.

The take away

The central message of Part 2 is that the Adaptive Economy presents many opportunities for a wide range of product and service providers. A selection are highlighted in Table 3. Successful organisations will manage their climate change risk exposure while tailoring their products and services to meet the new market needs that are emerging. Part 3 looks in more detail about how to prepare your business for success in the Adaptive Economy.

- Suppliers to
  - water & waste water utilities
  - major infrastructure projects
  - defense and border protection
- Food technologists, agricultural support
- Healthcare, pharmaceuticals
- Storm / flood protection
- Natural disaster response and recovery
- Innovators in:
  - transport (goods and passengers)
  - urban design & construction
  - clean energy / local energy

Table 3 – Key industries that may benefit from climate change

PART 3
PREPARING
YOUR BUSINESS

"Adapt or perish, now
as ever, is nature's
inexorable imperative."
H. G. Wells

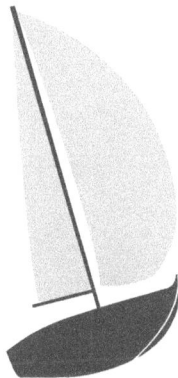

Chapter 8
Shades of Green – The Trouble with Corporate Sustainability

Around the globe, numerous companies are publicising and promoting their sustainability efforts. For example, flooring firm Interface systematically reviewed its product designs, production processes and supply chains to weed out fossil fuel dependence and create a compelling story around its cradle-to-cradle[22] solution for its products. On the other hand, General Electric bundled product lines and R&D connected with clean tech or energy efficiency under the Ecomagination branding. And British Petroleum some years ago changed their logo and tagline to Beyond Petroleum to promote their investments in renewable energy (before reverting to type some years later).

Research from the Association of Certified Chartered Accountants (ACCA) found that in 2011, 85 of the 100 largest companies listed on the Australian Securities Exchange reported on sustainability either as part of their annual report, or via a separate report.

Similar or better rates are found for the majors on other global stock markets. In the Australian review, 64 companies' sustainability reports were judged comprehensive and half of those were subject to external assurance.

While it's great that many companies are improving transparency on environmental matters, the breadth of reporting and what it actually says about a company's sustainability efforts often leaves a lot to be desired. As researcher Guy Pearse notes in his entertaining expose Greenwash, many sustainability reports look great printed on their Forestry Stewardship Council (FSC) certified recycled paper using soy based inks, but disguise the fact that the company's environmental footprint is actually increasing by failing to

---

22   Crade-to-Cradle means the company aims to reclaim its products when they are no longer wanted and then re-manufacture new products from the constituent materials.

report on supply chain impacts and/or only reporting on relative measures (for example emissions per widget) versus absolutes (total emissions).

Meanwhile, less discerning investors, customers and prospective employees may be duped by the feel-good hype into thinking that an organisation is doing some good for the environment when the true story is typically "more harm", or "slightly less harm" – if you're lucky.

In a classic case of "mutton dressed as lamb", many companies promote their comparatively token efforts related to sustainability while conducting operations that are anything but good for the environment.

For example, a favourite greenwash gimmick for the banking industry and other high profile services based organisations is to obtain high green ratings for their office tenancies.

In Australia this means 5 Star or 6 Star Green Star ratings as certified by the Green Building Council of Australia; in the US, Gold or Platinum LEED (Leadership in Energy and Environmental Design); and in the UK an Excellent or Outstanding BREEAM rating (Building Research Establishment Environmental Assessment Methodology).

Putting aside criticism of such rating tools in terms of what they actually achieve from an emissions reduction point of view, high green ratings on corporate property certainly make it look like an organisation is doing something positive for the environment. They are great at attracting talent too. Who wouldn't want to work in a smart new building with good indoor air quality while thinking this means they're doing a good green deed for the planet?

These types of green credentials are also fairly cheap these days: within the per-square-metre fit out budget of a typical bank it's relatively easy to achieve a premium green rating. And they provide something to crow about in the sustainability report.

However, as we saw in Part 1, many banks lend billions to the fossil fuel industry. In the scheme of things, any actual emissions reduction or other environmental benefit of a high green rating on their headquarters building will be dwarfed by the emissions associated with the financial support the institution is providing to facilitate the extraction, sale and/or use of fossil fuels.

But at least their executives can rest easy thinking that they're doing something good for the environment.

In another example, a number of airlines, starting with Virgin in 2008, have made test flights using aircraft powered by biofuel. Never mind that it's one flight amongst the thousands flown every day – according to the marketing hype it's apparently one short flight for Airline X, but one giant leap for mankind.

While the odd commercial flight has been undertaken using a fraction of biofuel mixed with conventional aviation fuel, conversion to 100% biofuels is a long way off. Whether or not this would actually result in a decrease in aviation-related greenhouse emissions would depend on the source of the biofuel. Destroying forests to make way for land to grow fuel crops could potentially increase net emissions.

Then there are the firms who proudly proclaim carbon neutrality, typically through the use of purchased offsets. Sometimes they've even been certified carbon neutral by a government scheme or by one of the organisations that have popped up in the last decade to service this new market. But for a majority, the certification at best covers Scope 1 and 2 emissions[23] that are directly attributable to the organisation. For example, the emissions associated with the diesel they use in their trucks and the electricity they consume in their office buildings and warehouses. Some may cover a subset of Scope 3 emissions that are reasonably easy to calculate, such as business travel or paper use.

In some cases the boundary defining the carbon neutral organisation is kept deliberately narrow: head office only, for example, and excluding manufacturing plants. What carbon neutrality typically doesn't cover are the emissions associated with a company's suppliers, or their suppliers' suppliers and so forth back to the extraction of the raw materials they need. It doesn't necessarily cover the electricity their landlord pays for the air conditioners and lifts running in the building. And it certainly doesn't cover the downstream emissions associated with their customers' and end consumers' use of the organisation's products or services.

Some would say it's the responsibility of each organisation and individual to limit their own emissions, but that's a bit of a cop out, particularly when

23   Refer to Chapter 12 for an explanation of the differences between Scope 1, 2 and 3 emissions.

it comes to organisations that make things or those that design and market products that are made by others.

Upstream supply and logistics chains can be extensive when traced right back to the raw materials. And at every stage, there are emissions or other environmental degradation involved in extracting, processing and transporting components. But the vast majority of "carbon neutral" organisations don't include these Scope 3 emissions in their offset calculations.

As for the downstream emissions and environmental impact of delivering a product or service to a customer, organisations that sell items to other businesses that are then incorporated into other products or processed further become part of someone else's upstream supply chain. But ultimately products and services are consumed by end users, be they businesses or individuals. And that consumption process over the lifecycle of a product/service can involve greater or lesser environmental harm depending on the way it has been designed.

Automobiles are an obvious example. A hybrid vehicle is generally more fuel efficient than the equivalent non-hybrid petrol or diesel version and if driven on the same routes and serviced correctly it will have lower operating emissions over its lifetime. And what happens to the car when it reaches the end of its life? Is it disassembled so that the majority of its materials can be recycled, or is it crushed and disposed of in landfill, or maybe unceremoniously dumped in a creek?

Even the consumption of services leaves an environmental footprint. A bank account, for example, involves the delivery of statements to the account holder. Paper statements delivered monthly have a higher footprint than those delivered quarterly. The selection of paper stock and envelopes changes the footprint. The delivery route of the postal worker and their mode of transport changes the footprint. Switching to electronic statements delivered via email notifications changes the footprint, but if the consumer then prints the statement on an inefficient domestic grade printer on chlorine-bleached non-recycled paper from a non-sustainable source and forgets to turn their computer or printer off afterwards, then the apparent benefits of this method may be reversed.

So organisations claiming carbon neutrality or other environmental benefits based solely or primarily on the footprint of their own operations are for the most part kidding themselves and misleading consumers.

Which raises an interesting point: what does it mean as a corporate citizen to be "green" or "sustainable" or "eco-friendly" or "good for the environment" anyway?

None of these words/phrases has a legal definition governing its use (in Australia). Although a government-backed carbon neutral standard exists[cxlvii] it is not mandatory. A number of competing private certification schemes exist, but these are of varying quality.

Similarly, as mentioned in Chapter 5, there are dozens of schemes that claim to vet or rate the environmental credentials of everything from paper and office supplies to computers and buildings. Some are broad and well researched in their scope and application; others turn out to be schemes dreamt up by industry associations to give a green stamp of approval that may make consumers think they're doing the right thing but lack clear evidence and metrics of the resulting environmental benefits.

For instance: calling an office building "green" because it has a high Green Star or LEED or BREEAM rating doesn't necessarily mean that the lifecycle greenhouse emissions and overall environmental degradation associated with that building are going to be less dastardly than the similarly sized building across the street. They could potentially be worse.

Typically, green building rating systems look at the designs and construction process and assign weighted points based on certain criteria. In Australia, for example, Green Star offers a point for having someone on the project team who has been to the Green Building Council's Green Star course, passed the exam, goes to a few refresher seminars each year and pays annual subscription fees to maintain their accreditation.

It offers points for having plenty of bicycle parking and associated lockers and showers, even if none of the buildings' occupants actually use them to reduce their associated commuting emissions. You can get an extra point by providing bicycle parking that is accessible by visitors to the building – perhaps a stretch too far for someone visiting a law firm or investment bank. It offers a certain number of points for the use of steel or concrete with a level of recycled content (regardless of the energy or transport intensity of the recycling process), yet potentially no more points for a building using sustainably-harvested timber as its primary building material.

I worked on a project involving a multi-story office building that had a glass roof and no landscaping or overhanging trees – it was built out to the boundary of the property. Therefore, any rain on the site fell exclusively on the clean roof, was collected in gutters and piped out of the building. The rainwater was pretty clean when it landed on the roof and was still pretty clean when it left the site, not having had the opportunity to collect any sediments. Yet that project received Green Star points for installing a "jellyfish" filter, which uses a membrane system to filter storm water from a site before it is discharged to the municipal storm water system. Paying a bit extra for the filter helped the project achieve a maximum 6 Star Green Star rating, which is what the client was seeking because a high Green Star rating equates to a premium on rental prices as it is valued by corporate tenants as an employee attractor.

Let it be noted though, that the rationale behind the various points in the green building rating schemes is generally well intentioned. It's just that intentions and reality don't always coincide.

So if the green building rating systems don't always help determine which of our buildings are less bad than others, then what will?

One technique that is potentially more accurate is Life Cycle Assessment (LCA). As the name suggests, LCA aims to assess the environmental impact of a building (or any other product or service) over every stage of its life cycle. But LCA is still in its infancy, with several potential methodologies and measurement techniques that are still under development. It's also really complicated.

What an emissions-focused LCA attempts to do is forecast (or track) all the greenhouse emissions associated with (take a deep breath):

- Extracting/obtaining the dozens of raw materials used to make the components. If you think about a building this could include iron ore, aggregate, limestone, water, various other metals, timbers, silica for glass, oil for plastics, wool for carpets, rubber, rare earths, gases, and so on.
- Transporting them to hundreds of factories around the world.
- Processing them into thousands of components such as iron girders and reinforcing cables, cement, concrete, lumber, glazing panels, ceiling tiles, lighting fixtures, electrical and control cabling, air conditioning ducts, cooling towers and so on. In many cases materials undergo intermediate processing and are then transported, sometimes multiple times, for final assembly.
- Transporting parts to the building site, often via several warehouses.

- Constructing the building (including the use of hundreds of tools and vehicles by sometimes thousands of construction workers over several years).

- Disposal of significant amounts of waste associated with the construction process, from excavation soil to off-cuts and component packaging.

- Subsequent to the construction of the building itself, each subsequent tenant will typically undertake their own fit out, demolishing and erecting partitions and changing the furniture.

- During occupation of the building there are significant emissions associated with the energy consumed, which will vary depending on the level of occupancy, hours of use, local weather (affecting heating and cooling energy), and how intensive the tenants' use of information technology is.

- Over the life of the building there are also emissions associated with cleaning, maintenance and replacement of plant, replenishment of air conditioning system refrigerants, and so on. The lobby, roof and even the facade may be replaced during the life of the building.

- Some methodologies also attempt to consider the emissions associated with occupants' commuting travel.

- Eventually, after a life span that hopefully exceeds 50 years, the building will be deemed no longer fit for purpose and will be demolished or extensively refurbished. Emissions will vary depending on how easily different materials can be extricated and recycled versus dumped and buried in a landfill.

As I said, LCA is somewhat complex.

So after all that, which building performs better – the one with the green rating or the one across the road? Without PhD grade, multi-disciplinary academic research on each building it's pretty difficult to say. If the "non green" building was made from reasonably locally sourced materials, has been well maintained, has had its air conditioning system and lighting upgraded from time to time to improve energy efficiency and, particularly, if its occupied lifespan is longer than the so-called "green" building, then its lifecycle emissions could be lower.

Of course, emissions are only one aspect of environmental impact. You should also consider the lifecycle associated with other important metrics such as water use, waste in all its forms – including, for example, the impact of the particular cleaning products discharged into the sewage system and the refrigerant gases in the air conditioning system; environmental damage caused by extraction and production of all the materials; plus any associated with the change of use of the site; and the health, safety and comfort of occupants.

Relative weightings for these assessments will depend on the site's geography and other factors: for example, water use impacts may be relatively less or more significant depending on the medium to long term water abundance of the locale. And for any staunch environmentalists who might be inclined to dismiss the importance of occupant health and comfort levels, bear in mind that this is a key factor that will maximise utilisation levels for the building: better a full building than one that is difficult to lease because occupants don't like working there.

It is said that the most sustainable building is the one that doesn't need to be built.

Prolonging the use of existing buildings rather than demolishing and replacing them is a critical first step.

Reducing the amount of floor space needed by promoting desk sharing and telecommuting schemes – which incidentally could reduce employee transport emissions – might be another.

The stark truth though is, that in working with organisations large and small, we've found that many corporate sustainability programs are little more than window dressing. That said, there are some well-intentioned initiatives like replacing vehicle fleets with hybrids, "green champions" running round offices switching off lights and PCs, use of carbon credits to offset emissions, installation of energy and water meters to better track usage and spot opportunities for efficiency, and the like.

They're the kind of initiatives that are generally focused on measurement and mitigation, but typically they have little accountability for meeting reduction targets, particularly when tougher economic conditions intervene. A lot of the "green initiatives" we see sound good on paper, and may be good in terms of the organisation's market or employment branding, but because none of it is based on robust Life Cycle Assessment, it's hard to say whether it is actually achieving any useful environmental outcomes.

In most firms it's hard to find transformative thinking about climate change and other macro-environmental issues. The sort of thinking that says, "hey, we are not in the right business", or, "actually, we could adapt this product/service or promote it to a new market to meet the challenge of climate change". That then, is the focus of Part 3.

Chapter 9
Crafting a Meaningful Sustainability Strategy for Your Business

There are a wealth of standards, data aggregators, buy-side analysts, consultancies and awards ceremonies geared up around corporate sustainability. It's possible to get an award for producing a sustainability report that is fully compliant with the Global Reporting Initiative's Corporate Social Responsibility (CSR) requirements, but have contents that on close examination indicate that the organisation has in fact substantially increased its carbon emissions.

This kind of thing can both slip under the radar, and not even be helpful in terms of investment decision-making, as it is not readily possible for a typical investor to digest the sustainability reports of several companies and determine which of them is better, or – as is more commonly the case – less bad for the environment.

Frustrated by this lack of objectivity and comparability, my colleagues and I have created the Adaptive Capability Maturity Model (AdaptiveCMM) to assess an organisation's level of preparedness for the Adaptive Economy.

We took a good look at what it would take to make an organisation resilient and sustainable in the 21st century and applied the Capability Maturity Model (CMM) methodology to this challenge.

So what is a CMM?

In the 1980s the US Defense Department's Software Engineering Institute looked for ways to help reduce the number of computer software development projects that were spiraling out of control, with sometimes massive time and budget over-runs and disappointing outcomes in terms of the functionality of the finished product.

It needed a tool to assess the capability of defense sub-contractors who were producing the software, before it awarded contracts. So the SEI researched the key processes that determined competence in producing software, and developed a diagnostic to assess how good (mature) a particular software development firm was at each of those disciplines.[cxlviii]

The fundamentals of a CMM involve breaking key processes into typically five maturity levels, from basic (basic) to best (sophisticated). Objectives are defined for each process and maturity level and a questionnaire / validation process developed to assess an organisation's level of attainment. The trick is understanding and weighting the factors that make a difference, since ultimately the CMM boils down to a number that represents the maturity level.

Since the 1980s CMMs have been applied to various other aspects such as Records Management, Human Resources Management and Risk Management. They are not only good ready reckoners about an organisation's competence in a particular domain, but are also very useful in determining a road map for an organisation that wants to get better at something. This is because once an organisation's current maturity level is understood, it's possible to identify what they need to do to get them to the next maturity level, with a fair amount of granularity.

They are also great at allowing organisations to baseline and track their progress, while potentially baselining themselves against other organisations in their industry or market.

In the AdaptiveCMM, we set out to develop a tool that would help our clients understand where they stood on their journey towards sustainability, that is, progress towards occupying the upper right hand quadrant of the Impact / Climate sensitivity matrix introduced in Chapter 2. We wanted to know a lot about our clients, and we divided the AdaptiveCMM into seven capability domains.

Based on our research, we believe truly resilient and sustainable organisations (Level 5 or Sophisticated on the CMM scale) need to exhibit the characteristics summarised in Table 4:

Governance, policy, decision-making and accountability	• Climate change and environmental considerations are integral to the organisation. • Formal governance structures are in place to achieve beneficial long-term natural capital management outcomes. • The organisation has an effective culture and processes to identify and adapt to new challenges.
Environmental impact measurement	• Comprehensive tools and processes are in place to measure and track all aspects of the organisation's environmental impact up and down the supply chain. • Lifecycle impacts of its products and services are understood, using appropriate, audited measurement standards.
Risk assessment	• Systematic and comprehensive climate change and environmental risk assessments are undertaken regularly, with the involvement of appropriately qualified experts, and are externally audited. • Environmental scanning processes are effective at detecting both the risks and opportunities associated with these issues.
Operational resilience	• Systematic business continuity and contingency plans and arrangements are in place covering the organisation's full supply chain, both for climate change and broader environmental risks.
Environmental impact mitigation	• The organisation's carbon footprint is neutral or positive up and down its supply chain. • Other environmental metrics such as water use and waste production are significantly lower than peer organisations. • Products, services and operations generally benefit the environment rather than harming it.
Stakeholder engagement	• The organisation takes an environmental leadership position in engagement with all stakeholder groups including staff, investors, its supply chain, customers, end users, government and the public. • It publicly provides full disclosure of its greenhouse gas emissions and environmental impact, risk exposure and mitigation efforts.
Adaptive capacity	• Comprehensive long term business planning takes into account the full range of impacts of climate change and other environmental risks. • The organisation produces the right products, the right way, at the right time for the right markets.

Table 4 – Capabilities of Truly Sustainable Organisations (Level 5)

This is the description of an organisation that is genuinely treading as lightly as possible on the planet, one which is actively leading other organisations, institutions and individuals on their sustainability journey, and which is producing products/services and serving markets in a manner that is equipped to deal with the challenges that climate change and other forms of environmental degradation are bringing.

While opportunities abound for short term profiteering, in the longer term these are the types of organisations that will thrive in the remainder of the 21st century.

At the other end of the scale, we decided that having maturity Level 1 (Basic) was inadequate given the number of organisations that still seem to dispute or deny the science of anthropogenic climate change, mostly because decarbonising may present a threat to their core business lines. Accordingly we created Level 0 (Unaware) to provide a starting point for such organisations. Characteristics of an Unaware organisation across the seven domains are summarised in Table 5.

Governance, policy, decision-making and accountability	• Key executives may deny the science of anthropogenic climate change. • There is no policy related to climate change or environmental sustainability. • Market / environmental scanning processes are limited • Executive remuneration is focused on short term financial outcomes.
Environmental impact measurement	• Not considered except directly in response to mandatory requirements.
Risk assessment	• Climate change and environmental impacts are not consciously considered in operational risk assessments except where required by law.
Operational resilience	• No expectation of change to status quo.
Environmental impact mitigation	• Measures not consciously pursued or implemented except indirectly to achieve cost savings or for compliance purposes.
Stakeholder engagement	• Messages (if any) related to climate change and environmental issues may attempt to deny or diminish the scientific consensus.
Adaptive capacity	• The organisation has no expectation of a change to status quo.

Table 5 – Capabilities of an "Unaware" Organisation (Level 0)

Between Level 0 and Level 5 are four intermediate stages, with differing expectations for each of the capability domains at each level. Of course, it is possible for an organisation to be more advanced in regards to certain specific domains compared to others, so the output of the diagnostic includes both the aggregate score and domain specific detail.

Figure 10 provides an overview of the AdaptiveCMM diagnostic.

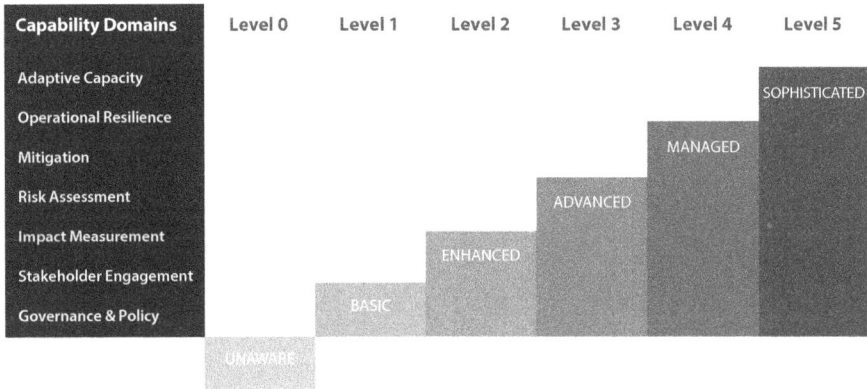

Figure 10 – The AdaptiveCMM: overview

Part of being a sustainable organisation means knowing your supply chain is also sustainable. In this case the AdaptiveCMM can be used by procurement teams – by applying it to companies that provide their organisation with products and services. Generally, this involves an initial base-lining exercise with major suppliers, to ascertain what level each is at and their relative strengths and weaknesses. The procurement team can then engage with poorly performing suppliers, providing encouragement and in some cases training or other support to help them improve.

Underperforming suppliers are then advised that in order to retain their clients' business they need to achieve a minimum Level in the Adaptive CMM within a particular timeframe. Meanwhile, a minimum Adaptive CMM rating becomes a requirement for new suppliers seeking to do business with the organisation. Periodically, suppliers can be reassessed to ascertain their progress, with their disclosures audited if necessary.

In this way an organisation can gradually ratchet its suppliers through the Adaptive CMM Levels as highlighted in Figure 11. Of course, this process involves a potential overhead for suppliers and works most effectively when the lead organisation has considerable buying power and is large relative to the size of most of its suppliers.

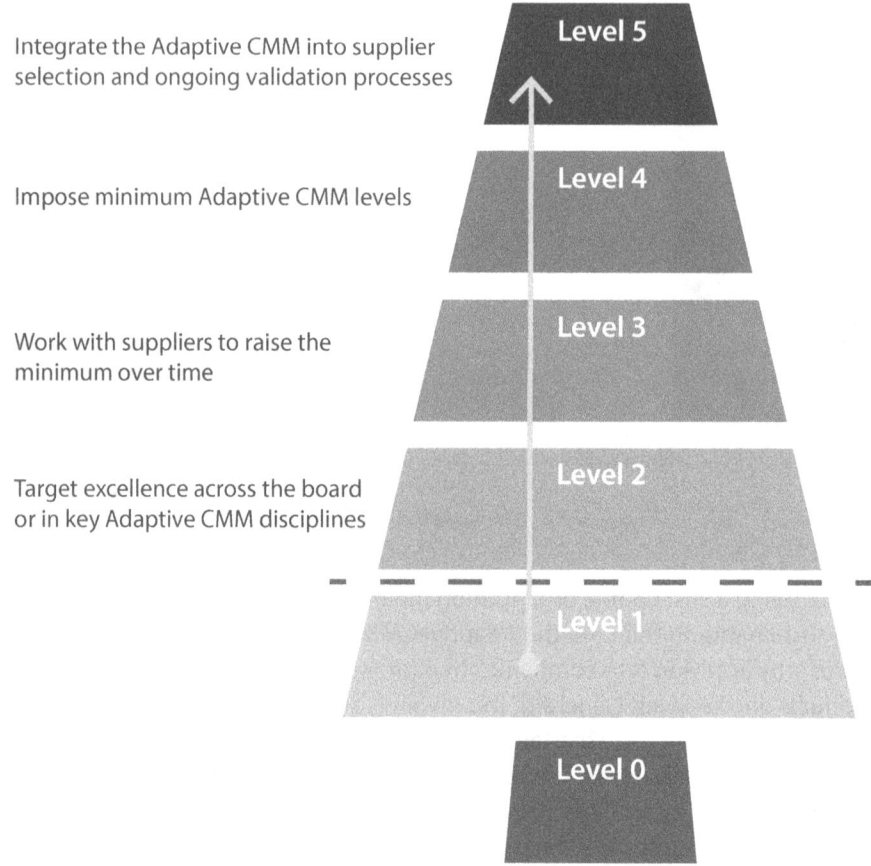

Integrate the Adaptive CMM into supplier selection and ongoing validation processes — **Level 5**

Impose minimum Adaptive CMM levels — **Level 4**

Work with suppliers to raise the minimum over time — **Level 3**

Target excellence across the board or in key Adaptive CMM disciplines — **Level 2**

Level 1

Level 0

Figure 11 – Use of the Adaptive CMM to improve corporate procurement outcomes

The following chapters highlight in more detail the characteristics of organisations that score well on the AdaptiveCMM.

Chapter 10
Good Governance

As a strategic risk management issue, it is essential that responsibilities and accountabilities for monitoring and controlling an organisation's approach to climate change and environmental matters be considered as a core corporate governance requirement. Particularly for exposed sectors including the fossil fuel industry and organisations that will bear the brunt of climate change impacts such as coastal infrastructure providers (and the bankers and insurers for these entities) it is imperative that climate and environmental issues are addressed at board level, with responsibilities and accountabilities clearly defined.

But even for less exposed industries and geographies, any larger organisation should have appropriate governance mechanisms in place to help it avoid risk and capture value from the transition to the Adaptive Economy.

Typically, depending on the size and nature of the organisation, the following might be expected:

- A board-endorsed policy related to environmental and business sustainability, which should:
  - Acknowledge the importance of avoiding adverse environmental impact in all its forms;
  - Establish objective targets related to environmental impact reduction and mitigation (both operationally and up and down the organisation's supply chains);
  - Direct the use of shadow pricing of environmental impacts in business cases where external pricing mechanisms for such impacts do not yet exist (or where such external pricing does not adequately reflect the cost of the impacts);[24]

---

24   For example, a number of energy companies have incorporated a shadow carbon price of USD$20 or more per tonne into their business case models when assessing new explorations.

- Provide principles for risk assessment and management of environmental considerations (as discussed elsewhere in this book);
- Outline associated accountabilities for management and employees; and
- Identify strategic opportunities related to climate change.

- The policy should then cascade into artifacts such as position descriptions and performance agreements, with a percentage of senior executives' remuneration packages at risk against the achievement of specific targets.

- Climate and environmental matters should be introduced to the board agenda, initially in the context of introducing the policy and, in turn, in relation to the risk and opportunity assessment discussed in later chapters.

- Staff should be invited to provide input into the policy, potentially using workshops to facilitate their contribution.

- Where risk levels are non-trivial, create a board sub-committee to focus on strategic climate and environmental risks.

- Appointment of a Chief Sustainability Officer (CSO) or similar senior position charged with improving the organisation's environmental governance, leadership, resource efficiency and revenue generation through environmentally-related initiatives.

- Implement a training and awareness program to better educate management and staff about climate change and environmental issues, specific risks, and opportunities including mitigation, adaptation and product/service transformation.

- The introduction of a broadly applied Environmental Risk Management system in accordance with the ISO 14000 series of international standards and/or other credible systems to minimise the risks of environmental issues.

- Development and publication of a Sustainability Report, based on a reputable standard.

- Internal and external auditing/assurance of sustainability / environmental reporting and the measures and achievements it documents.

At this point it is worthwhile reiterating the point made in the previous chapter: that a well-composed sustainability report does not make a sustainable organisation (even if it wins a corporate sustainability award). Critical thought is necessary to determine which activities will be most beneficial in terms of both minimising the environmental impact of an organisation and ensuring its responsible economic success over the medium to longer term.

The Global Reporting Initiative (GRI) was established to develop a standardised approach to sustainability reporting and has produced detailed guidelines to inform organisations.[cxlix] However, research by the Australian Council of Superannuation Investors (ACSI) and the Australian Financial Services Council (FSC) has criticised the consistency of such reporting even when GRI guidelines are applied, with reports often weighted towards a focus on good news reporting and patchy coverage of bad news. In turn, the FSC has published its own guidance to "facilitate the integration of ESG factors into investment decision making processes".[cl]

Ultimately, the success of any governance program often boils down to whether the main protagonists – the board and senior executive of the organisation – actually see value in the exercise. When they are ambivalent or in some cases even hostile, environmental governance becomes just another "tick the box" compliance exercise. However, if there is a critical mass of senior personnel who "get" the risks and opportunities presented by the Adaptive Economy, then the organisation's sustainability program will flourish.

But it doesn't stop with the executives. A key characteristic of an organisation is its Absorptive Capacity – its routines for identifying and assimilating valuable knowledge about the environment and its changing nature.[cli] Research by Cohen and Levinthal[clii] and others has found that "organisations that adopt a regular rhythm of strategic change outperform those that change irregularly".

As the name suggests, Absorptive Capacity has characteristics like a sponge's highly porous construction, enormous surface area and ability to wick up moisture. In this case, an organisation with effective Absorptive Capacity will have a broad arsenal of information gathering mechanisms – not just formal market scanning, competitor, industry and SWOT analyses undertaken by corporate Marketing and Strategy teams, but a range of informal techniques and a more expansive variety of sources of potential insight. These may include the organisation's engagement with employees, industry groups, customers, government, academia and other research organisations, environmental groups and other providers of new ideas and insights, and the use of multiple media. We'll talk more about stakeholder engagement in the next chapter, but suffice to say one of the essentials is that the organisation should not limit its sources of insight to the extent that it becomes myopic.

Absorbing information is just one part of Absorptive Capacity. Organisations need to be able to assimilate, filter and in turn make plans and act on the resulting insights, while ensuring appropriate feedback loops are in place to assess the outcomes of their decisions. They must avoid applying inherent biases in the evaluation of new information. In other words, it's critical to approach new ideas with an open mind and avoid subjective assessments.

Organisations also need appropriate incentives to be implemented to encourage actions that are aligned with the profit-making imperative of a company, but not at the expense of the environment.

One of the fundamental limitations of corporate finance (at least when it comes to dealing with market externalities such as climate change, environmental degradation or remediation of mine sites) is the notion of shareholder value maximization (SVM), which has been traditionally accepted economic wisdom for the past quarter century or so.

The return on equity calculation for a shareholder is based on income from a stream of dividends paid out of the firm's net profits, and/or the expectation of capital gain (that is, an increasing share price that can be sold at some future point for more than the investor paid for it).

Though subject to the vagaries of market sentiment and other emotion driven pricing decisions, the stock price of a company is generally loosely based on the present (discounted) value of future expected returns. For the price to increase, then those returns also need to increase. In the minds of many investors this means, if not quarter on quarter then at the very least year on year. An example of how this plays out can be seen when a particular company's stock price gets hammered when it announces a record profit that nevertheless falls short of analysts' expectations.

Therefore, an obstacle to significant organisational transformation is the fact that profits may decrease, or indeed, the business may run at a loss for a period of time. This is likely for some firms given the types of transformations that may be necessary to help them prepare for the Adaptive Economy. Ensuring significant investors and debt holders are on-side with the proposed transformation is essential.

As such, a critical element of corporate governance is executive remuneration. Recent empirical research has begun to question the maxim of shareholder value maximisation, with a good summary published in 2014 by James

Montier of Boston-based asset management firm Grantham Mayo van Otterloo (GMO).[cliii]

Montier and other commentators argue convincingly that, far from maximising value to shareholders, a focus on SVM actually leads to sub-optimal outcomes not just for a firm's equity owners, but also for society at large. In fact the principal beneficiaries of SVM seem to be the very chief executives hired to maximise value to shareholders.

In the years since SVM as a corporate maxim became widespread, Chief Executive Officers' pay and remuneration to senior employees in the investment banking sector has ballooned relative to ordinary employees, while at the same time both CEO tenure, and companies' tenure in major market indices like the US S&P500 has declined dramatically, propagating a short-term focus. This has in turn concentrated wealth in the hands of a few, with the top 1% in the United States and other western democracies capturing more than double the share of wealth compared with the post-World War II period before SVM took over boardroom thinking.

Further, the short term focus has led to under-investment, with cost cutting and an increase in the percentage of free cash flows returned to shareholders bleeding many firms of the resources needed to develop the longer term capabilities to respond to changing conditions. While this obviously has implications for the economic sustainability and survivability of individual firms, SVM thinking has also pervaded the public sector, with fewer politicians prepared to undertake nation-building initiatives that may risk short term popularity due to their initial costs or impacts on the electorate.

Montier also cites research assessing the optimal level of executive compensation, finding that beyond a certain level of remuneration, people become so fixated on the pay itself that they lose sight of the job in hand and performance drops off.

Accordingly, in order to ensure corporate outcomes that are good for the long-term health of the company, the environment and the wider society, it is critical that executive remuneration is set at appropriate levels and linked to the right things. This is admittedly easier said than done, and beyond the scope of this book. However, in general the use of longer-term contracts, a more balanced scorecard of key performance indicators for senior executives and mechanisms to link current decisions to future outcomes (both financial and non-financial) are recommended.

It can be useful to look at the example of many privately owned (non-listed) companies, particularly those under the long-term control of the original founders or their family. Montier draws on research showing double the level of investment in such firms compared to publically listed companies, even when comparing relatively like-for-like businesses.

In summary, effective governance for the Adaptive Economy requires:

- The appointment of a board and senior executive team who understand the need and opportunities for a broad transformation catalysed by climate change.

- An organisational culture that seeks out and is receptive to new ideas and displays high levels of Absorptive Capacity.

- Executive remuneration structures that reward a long term view and environmentally sensitive approach.

- Sympathetic owners, particularly institutional investors, who are prepared to accept a period of potentially lower returns and higher costs and, perhaps, a future of diminished profitability once the full costs of the organisation's use of natural capital are accounted for.

Chapter 11
Engaging with Stakeholders

Businesses influence the lives and shape the thinking of many people –
billions in the case of corporate behemoths such as FMCG (fast moving
consumer goods) giants Unilever and Proctor and Gamble, global restaurateur
McDonalds, retailer Walmart, beverage firms Coke and Pepsi, entertainment/
media brands Disney and Comcast and technology leaders such as
Google and Apple.

These and similar firms are superbly positioned to influence the shift towards
a more sustainable future (or not as the case may be), in terms of the type,
design, materials sourcing and manufacture of the products and services they
offer, and the way they communicate appropriate environmental messages.
Indeed, some of the companies mentioned above are actively seeking a
leadership position, announcing various measures to begin to decarbonise
their operations.

Of course customers are only one group of an organisation's stakeholders. A
company (particularly in the case of medium to large firms) is influenced by
and has the opportunity to influence many other groups in different ways
(both positive and negative) including:

- its board of directors;
- investors / shareholders;
- industry association(s);
- advertisers / media partners;
- governments and specific political parties;
- the general public / society at large; and
- philanthropic, scientific and educational organisations it
  supports or opposes.

An organisation's communications channels with these constituencies are
varied and can include, beyond the product/service itself, media such as its:

- packaging and point of sale messaging;
- traditional advertising (TV, radio, print, billboards, direct mail, point of sale, etc.);
- web site;
- social media presence;
- public relations and advertorial content;
- product placement marketing;
- political lobbying;
- annual reports / sustainability reports;
- investor briefings; and
- disclosures to organisations such as the investor-oriented Carbon Disclosure Project or government equivalents.

And as for the types of communications of an environmental nature, these may potentially include, amongst other things:

- Specific messages about the organisation's own environmental impact (or that of its products and services) and what is being done to reduce it.
- More relative or comparative statements about environmental performance (such as 'product X involves y% less greenhouse emissions than product Z' or comparisons to an industry average).
- Exhortations to others to improve their own environmental performance, occasionally with an altruistic motivation, but more often with an underlying marketing intent (as in, buy our product to reduce your environmental impact, or, more insidiously, buy our product because our marketing implies that it will help reduce your impact).
- Subtle and not so subtle messages that imply good corporate environmental performance which disguise actual negative impact. We've previously discussed the approach of banking organisations trumpeting their green office buildings while simultaneously lending to new fossil fuel projects.
- Communications that undermine established environmental science to defend or encourage consumption of products or services that contribute environmental harm.

Given the complexity of these stakeholder interactions, an organisation seeking to position itself for the Adaptive Economy should consider the following:

First and somewhat obviously, it should aim to put itself in the shoes of the various stakeholder groups that may be affected by its activities and products/services. Undertaking a stakeholder analysis for each constituency can help identify how its actions or potential actions will be perceived. In addition to likely stakeholder sentiment today, it is critical to project how the organisation could be perceived in the future in the face of various tipping points, such as a marked shift in the public's concern about environmental issues (perhaps precipitated by a major environmental disaster); or a change in government. We look more at potential tipping points in Chapter 13.

A useful means of assessing the appropriateness of an organisation's actions is the so-called "front page test", in which the implications of its actions appearing as a lead item in a major news broadcast are considered. How would each stakeholder group perceive the organisation's approach to the considerations listed in Figure 12, should they be exposed by a media organisation? If the answers are generally negative, this may serve as a catalyst for action.

Organisation's performance...	Today's stakeholder sentiment			Future sentiment assuming tipping points		
Environmental impact of its or its suppliers': • Materials extraction use (including extent of recycled materials) • Land use impacts • Production processes • Energy and water intensity and sources • Waste, waste treatment, and recycling of waste • Transportation footprint • Use of its products / services • Product / service end of life treatment	Strongly Negative	Neutral	Strongly Positive	Strongly Negative	Neutral	Strongly Positive
Resilience of its: • Supply chains • Own operations	Strongly Negative	Neutral	Strongly Positive	Strongly Negative	Neutral	Strongly Positive
Resilience of its: • Environmental impact • Susceptibility to environmental tipping points • Impact on the health and welfare of their users and the broader community	Strongly Negative	Neutral	Strongly Positive	Strongly Negative	Neutral	Strongly Positive
Integrity / scientific accuracy of its: • Marketing • Lobbying	Strongly Negative	Neutral	Strongly Positive	Strongly Negative	Neutral	Strongly Positive
Integrity / scientific accuracy of its: • Staff • Suppliers' staff • Communities with which it and its suppliers interact	Strongly Negative	Neutral	Strongly Positive	Strongly Negative	Neutral	Strongly Positive

Figure 12 – Stakeholder "front page test" diagnostic

Over time, it is expected companies that embrace the principles of the Adaptive Economy will work to ensure that their environmental and social impact is positively perceived by stakeholder groups. On the flip side, social media is facilitating increasing scrutiny around the authenticity of organisations' claims.

Unfortunately, gains that satisfy one set of stakeholders with regards to the organisation's environmental performance may disappoint the interests of other stakeholders who may be more concerned with, say, short term financial performance (or in the case of industry group stakeholders the willingness of an organisation to uphold the party line).

At this point the ethics of the organisation's actions should be examined. Recalling Chapter 10, the leadership team of firms wishing to be at the forefront of the Adaptive Economy may choose to reduce the emphasis on traditional metrics of organisational success in order to make a principled contribution to the safety and equitable-prosperity of both current and future generations of people, plus advance their contribution to protecting and enhancing the quality and biodiversity of the natural environment.

In the sections below we will look at a several examples of stakeholder communications we expect to see leaders in the Adaptive Economy engaging in.

Customer engagement

A key step involves a commitment to honest and unvarnished communications with consumers and other stakeholders. Over the years a variety of legislation has been introduced to force organisations to disclose more information about the contents of their products. Think of food labeling requiring reasonably complete disclosure of ingredients and country of origin, or fast food chains required to include the calorific content of their meals on menus. In some countries, such measures are only providing a fraction of the information that might be useful to help consumers make well-informed decisions.[25]

Indeed, in many cases, while compliance may be to the letter of the law, consumers remain thoroughly confused or manipulated. A good example is Australia's recently amended country of origin legislation, which frequently

---

25   In Australia, for example, there is no legal obligation to list the constituent elements of compound ingredients such as "cheese" or "soy sauce" if the compound ingredient is less than 5% of the food product's content.[cliv]

saw the legitimate use of the near-meaningless moniker "Made in Australia from Local and Imported Ingredients", when the "Australian" component of the process could sometimes be as trivial as the packaging.

Just as food retailers are often now obliged to provide cost per quantity pricing to help consumers navigate differing package sizes, it may be that labeling standards in the future allow comparison of factors relevant to specific products or services such as:

- Lifecycle GHG emissions per unit (including transport emissions)
- Lifecycle water use per unit
- Percentage use of recycled content (for both the product if applicable and its packaging)
- End of life take back arrangements for consumer durables (including the percentage that winds up in landfill if such facilities are used by the consumer)
- Metrics around the sustainability of growing and harvesting methods for different types of food

This amount of information may overwhelm many consumers, which is why eco-labels and associated product certification schemes have become popular (as discussed in Part 2). However, with literally hundreds of competing eco-labels vying for attention, it is all too easy for consumers to switch off entirely or to fall for labels that look familiar (such as the generic triangular recycling symbol in Figure 13, the use of which is un-policed, not subject to trademark protection and may mean nothing about the product or packaging on which it is displayed).

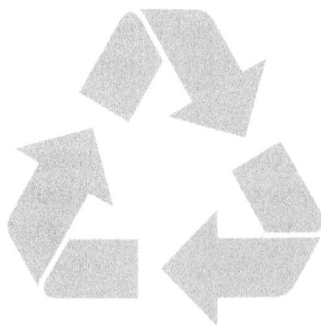

Figure 13– The ubiquitous but largely meaningless recycling symbol

While we expect to see more government action in the eco-label space to impose well-considered standards, independent certification and enforcement, it is also acknowledged that governments tend to concentrate on minimum standards. Industry-led or independent standards have traditionally sought to provide market differentiation above those minima, raising the bar beyond mandatory compliance. Accordingly, in future we may see tighter enforcement by governments of the ISO 1402X series of standards relating to the application and use of environmental labels.

Government

Firms with appropriate mass, or industry groups representing smaller organisations can bring considerable weight to bear and influence government policy. In fact, in some jurisdictions, lobbyists working on behalf of major corporates actually draft Bills that are then presented to Parliament, often ensuring favourable outcomes.[clv] In other countries, corporate donations (and in some cases bribes) to political parties or individual politicians help influence policy and legislative outcomes. Unfortunately, such measures typically further the profitability motives of the corporations, often at the expense of the environment.

Organisations in the Adaptive Economy will use their influence with governments to foster a constructive dialogue about environmental protection, including the planned transformation (rather than protection) of climate-exposed industries.

Owners and investors

As discussed in the previous chapter on Governance, a key stakeholder group that needs to be engaged with is the owners of a company (in the case of a publicly-listed company, its shareholders). A company that is to thrive in the Adaptive Economy should fully value its investments in natural capital and should make compensatory payments towards remediation (such as so-called offset projects) even as it searches for ways to reduce its environmental impact. This may reduce returns, so the company needs to take its investors on the journey.

On the flip side, major institutional investors such as fund managers and banks can play the opposite role: applying effective screening criteria to pick stocks or back projects that limit environmental impact; encouraging the organisations in which they invest to take steps to reduce their impact; and divesting from firms that continue to undertake damaging activities.

A range of analytical providers already produce reports targeted at fund managers allowing them to assess the environmental, social and governance (ESG) performance of the stocks in their portfolios. For example, global stock index provider MSCI provides tools allowing the annual greenhouse gas emissions and fossil fuel reserves of a portfolio to be estimated.

Many institutional investors are becoming more discerning in their investment screening, incorporating specialist ESG risk teams into their enterprise risk management functions and applying increasingly stringent filters alongside traditional risk measures such as credit exposure and sovereign risk. For corporates seeking investment funds, therefore, it is becoming increasingly important to manage the quality of the ESG information available to investors and, in turn, to ensure that information is attractive given the filtering now being undertaken.

Growth in the divestment movement (refer to Chapter 2) is expected to spur changes in the way people invest and banks operate. Strong growth in the renewables sector, which is likely to continue for several decades, has seen so-called fossil-free stock indices outperform broader benchmarks in both the United States and Australia.[clvi]

Another critical aspect of disclosure to investors is the organisation's vulnerability or exposure to the various impact categories discussed in Chapter 3. The World Economic Forum's Global Risks Report consistently ranks environmental risks, including climate change in its top 10,[clvii] and a 2011 report by Mercer, "Climate Change Scenarios – Implications for Strategic Asset Allocation",[clviii] which was commissioned by a number of large investment managers, notes "it is widely acknowledged that climate change will have a broad-ranging impact on economies and financial markets over the coming decades".

In addition, various high profile reports have recently been issued from national and supranational organisations on the topic of unburnable carbon. For example the Bank of England announced in December 2014 that it will examine the vulnerability of fossil fuel assets to the stability of the financial markets.

The public

George Marshall's recent foray into the psychology of climate change, "Don't Even Think About It", exposes both the difficulty of changing entrenched world views and the challenge of creating and sustaining interest amongst the public about a topic that is complex and ephemeral, lacks a villain and seems remote in time and place to most people. As such, even a large consumer brand with good intentions and deep pockets for an extended marketing campaign on the topic is likely to face attacks from both green groups and deniers of climate change, not to mention apathy from many sectors of the community.

While we believe it is critical that companies do communicate directly to the public about the risks of climate change, the need to change our energy systems, methods of food production, approaches to construction, consumption and so on, we think the best way to do it is by telling stories.

Organisations that can construct an honest, personal and compelling narrative about how they are going about transforming themselves, their products and services, their supply chains and the communities with which they interact are likely to be looked on more favourably by potential customers and less likely to be targeted by green groups.

As we saw in Chapter 8, any sense of hypocrisy in such a narrative will likely be seized on as another example of greenwash, in some cases by competitors in a classic case of the proverbial pot calling the kettle black. Therefore, the narrative should articulate what stage of its journey the organisation is on, acknowledge the breadth of its environmental impact and talk about what it is doing to reduce it and prepare itself for a climate changing world.

Sometimes, even companies that believe they are genuinely trying to do the right thing face stakeholder challenges. For example, wind farm developers who are trying to provide a renewable energy source to reduce dependence on fossil fuels frequently face opposition both from local communities who are concerned with the visual impact and potential health impacts from the noise (to humans and/or grazing livestock); and environmentalists who worry about deaths of birds, bats or insects that fly into or near the turbines.

Naturally, various research has been commissioned to attempt to allay such concerns. However, results from studies can vary given methodological differences or inability in some cases to control other variables that might influence the outcomes. In the common absence of an independent referee who is willing to fund the research, the costs are typically borne by one or other side of the debate, raising accusations of potential bias (where the results favour the position of the commissioning entity). Regardless of the actual independence and validity of the research, such accusations can undermine its usefulness. And as with many new technologies, it can take many years to produce a compelling longitudinal data set to comprehensively dispel (or confirm) assertions of public health or other risks.

A useful data set would allow comparison with alternate forms of generation. Wind farms may be visually intrusive, but hardly when compared with a coal fired power station, let alone an open cut coal mine. Ditto noise, health and wildlife impacts. Coal dust is known to have a deleterious effect on the health of nearby residents, for example. Insects are attracted to gas flares at well heads and refineries literally like a moth to a flame. When a balanced comparative assessment is presented, any negative impacts of wind farms may seem trivial in relative terms.

Similarly, organisations should compare their own environmental impact in both absolute and relative terms, with reference to a range of substitute products or activities.

Chapter 12
Measurement and Mitigation

The old adage, you can't manage what you don't measure, is particularly pertinent when it comes to sustainability. The two domains of environmental impact measurement and, in turn, mitigation – the reduction of that impact – go hand in hand. But what does an organisation's environmental impact consist of anyway, and how do you set about measuring it?

Basically an impact assessment aims to calculate an organisation's (or in some cases a product's) direct and indirect use of natural capital assets (i.e. inputs provided by nature) and/or its contribution to one or more forms of pollution. For example, a greenhouse gas (GHG) emissions assessment concentrates on measuring the emission of human-made GHGs as a result of an organisation's activities.

GHGs include carbon dioxide, methane and a number of others as defined by the United Nations Framework Convention on Climate Change (UNFCCC) and embodied in the GHG Protocol – a global measurement standard hammered out as part of the Kyoto Protocol agreement. GHG measurement for organisations has been around for long enough that the International Standards Organisation has had time to turn it into ISO 14064, so we'll skate over the fundamentals fairly quickly.

Under the measurement scheme, GHG emissions are divided into three groups, known as "scopes", which define the organisational boundary of the data being collected.

For many services based organisations that rent their office accommodation and have no other owned-plant, it is relatively simple to calculate direct emissions based on use on use of fuel (e.g. by fleet vehicles or diesel used in generators owned by the organisation). These are called "Scope 1" emissions under the Protocol. For industrial firms, consumption or creation of the full range of GHGs needs to be considered.

Scope 2 emissions are associated with purchased electricity, heat or steam. These are generated by a third party organisation and it's necessary to understand both the fuel source(s) (black coal, brown coal, oil, gas, wind, hydro, solar, nuclear, etc.) and in what proportion they are used, to in turn decide upon an appropriate coefficient to apply to consumption units such as kWh and determine the associated emissions. Transmission losses given the distance between the point of generation and the point of use should also be considered. Fortunately, many state governments have taken the guesswork out of this process and publish official coefficients, typically expressed as kg of carbon dioxide equivalent per kWh.

Here it's worthwhile explaining the word "equivalent" in this context. You may recall in the breakout box at the end of the Introduction we talked about the global warming potential (GWP) of a particular greenhouse gas. Carbon dioxide has been assigned a GWP of one. Other greenhouse gases have values that determine their warming impact relative to that of carbon dioxide. The phrase carbon dioxide equivalent (CO_2e) simply aggregates all types of greenhouse gas emissions associated with a particular activity, weights them according to their respective GWPs and expresses them in one simple measure.

Finally, Scope 3 emissions deal with emissions arising because of the organisation's activities, but which are not within the organisation's control. This is where it gets a bit complicated, because, as touched on in Chapter 8, at its logical extent it involves understanding the emissions associated with every step of your organisation's upstream supply chain right back to the extraction of the raw materials and all intermediate processing steps. And not just main suppliers, but everything from office supplies and computers to your use of copy paper, taxis and flights. Ironically, these latter categories are often easier because corporate stationery and travel suppliers have jumped on the bandwagon and now typically provide clients reporting on at least the greenhouse emissions associated with their usage levels.

If you're considering the footprint of a product or service, you also need to follow the supply chain downstream and look at the emissions associated with all life cycle stages including shipping and distribution (including packaging), the lifetime use of the product and end of life disposal.

Unfortunately the term "supply chain" is fairly misleading, suggesting as it does a linear process with the totality of one organisation's output forming the whole of another's inputs. Generally, however, an organisation will have dozens, hundreds or in some cases thousands of suppliers and in turn will sell its goods and services to many different customers. Supply chain analysis quickly becomes complex.

The bad news is that fully determining Scope 3 emissions and undertaking a full product Life Cycle Assessment can be extremely challenging. In some cases the science and standards are still developing around measuring the impact of different activities. The process also involves the cooperation and effort of numerous organisations who must all be consistently applying a common measurement framework.

However, proxy methods exist, such as the input output method, which in Australia is based on national accounts data maintained by the Australian Bureau of Statistics (ABS) and converted to emissions metrics by research groups such as the University of Sydney's Integrated Sustainability Analysis (ISA) team.[clix] This method involves providing a detailed set of accounts showing expense categories. The dollar spend on each item is converted to approximate GHG emissions derived from ISA's database, which in turn is linked to the country's national emissions figures and moderated to avoid double counting. The idea is that one organisation's Scope 3 emissions represent other entities' Scope 1 and 2 emissions and the divisions avoid double counting when compiling national-level greenhouse accounts.

But that's just greenhouse gas emissions. Other important environmental footprint indicators may include, depending on the organisation and also on its operating locations:

- Water use. In addition to understanding how much water is used by an organisation (and its supply chain), other considerations are where that water comes from and what other environmentally sensitive sources might be available. For example, how much water is lost from its sites as runoff following rain? Could it be harvested and used, even if only for non-potable applications? Would that have a deleterious impact on other potential uses of that runoff?

- Waste in all its forms, including solid, liquid and gaseous, covering both the amount of waste produced and how much of it is usefully recycled. Issues to consider include:

  - Waste water and runoff that is discharged to municipal storm water reticulation, adjacent land or the nearest watercourse (treated and untreated).

- How much packaging waste is generated, both for individual units of the organisation's products and also for bulk packaging, at each stage of the chain. What is the mix of readily biodegradable or recyclable packaging versus waste that will wind up as landfill or litter?

- End of life product disposal. Whether it's envelopes for bank statements (and for that matter the statements themselves), used batteries, discarded cigarette butts, mobile phones, an old car or building, product waste is a growing scourge. How is consumer turnover and disposal of the product measured?

- Discharge of polluted water, even if it is as apparently innocuous as the more saline sea water expelled by a coastal desalination plant. Larger plants, particularly when installed in relatively enclosed bays, can increase the salinity of the local water, potentially affecting marine life.

- Release of chemical waste into the atmosphere.

- Other forms of pollution such as:

  - Soil contamination: when chemicals such as hydrocarbons, heavy metals, herbicides, pesticides and chlorinated hydrocarbons are released by spill or underground leakage.

  - Radioactive contamination.

  - Thermal pollution: temperature change in natural water bodies caused by human influence. This is becoming problematic as buildings and industry increasingly use a river or harbour as a free heat exchanger to cut down on their use and associated costs of energy and potable water use.

  - Visual pollution: evidence of industrial activity or waste products on the natural landscape.

  - Noise pollution: from roadway, aircraft, industrial and other non-natural noise sources.

  - Light pollution: including over-illumination that may affect the nocturnal activities of animals or cause astronomical interference.

- Other environmental impacts as appropriate to the organisation's operations such as:

  - Resource depletion: forestry, fisheries stocks, mining, depletion of soils or water supplies, etc.

- Environmental degradation: land clearing, habitat loss, species extinction, etc.
- Measures of resource depletion and other environmental degradation such as loss of biodiversity that take account of the operations of all upstream suppliers (back to raw materials extraction) and downstream activities (including lifecycle product use and end of life disposal/recycling).

Basically, almost every human activity has environmental consequences and while many are negligible in isolation, our growing population leads to significant collective impact.

While it is possible to collect and collate measurement data in a spreadsheet, it becomes unwieldy for an organisation of any significant size. A number of developers have developed computer software and services to assist organisations with calculating their environmental impacts in terms of GHG emissions and other metrics. Apart from the obvious benefits of a well designed database in keeping impact data in order, such systems can provide other advantages including:

- Automated data collection. Some systems tap into smart energy and water meters, automatically upload data from utility providers and capture common Scope 3 service providers' data including business flights, taxis, fleet usage, paper, waste/recycling metrics and so on.

- Real time monitoring and management of facilities. Some systems provide alerts if particular metrics exceed preset values. For example, knowing that water or energy use had suddenly spiked in supply to a building's chiller plant might be indicative of a hot day, but it could also indicate a leak or other fault condition, enabling remedial action to be taken quickly.

- More granular monitoring. Contemporary buildings and facilities are generally designed with a number of sensors and sub-meters for electricity and water use, in addition to the primary meter (from which the utility determines and invoices usage). Tracking such data in a spreadsheet would be extremely onerous, but with a system capturing the data automatically it can be used to identify issues and manage performance more precisely and quickly.

- Traceability and auditability of the coefficients used to translate, for example, an organisation's business flight or taxi records into estimated GHG emissions.

Mitigation targets

Armed with this information an organisation can start to understand how it can reduce its impact and what changes and innovations will generate the best bang for buck environmentally. It can use its measurement data to benchmark against peer organisations, track progress towards impact reduction, targets and communicate its success to current and potential customers, investors and other stakeholders. As awareness of environmental issues grows, more customers and regulators will be demanding comprehensive environmental impact data.

In setting mitigation targets for greenhouse gases, organisations should seek to match or exceed the pace of emissions reduction (on an absolute basis) that has been agreed at international levels in order to attempt to keep the level of global warming to two degrees Celsius or less. Given the long-lived nature of major greenhouse gases, this has been simplified to a global carbon "budget" of around one trillion tonnes (1,000,000,000,000 tonnes) of human emissions since the start of the industrial revolution (net of emissions absorbed by carbon sinks). Around 2010 we hit the half-way point, with about 500 billion tonnes added, at a current rate of over 10 billion per annum (and growing).

The UN IPCC has calculated that to stick within the two degrees warming limit, annual global emissions must peak by 2020, fall to less than 50% of current levels by 2040, and be close to zero by 2070, as highlighted in the graph in Figure 14:

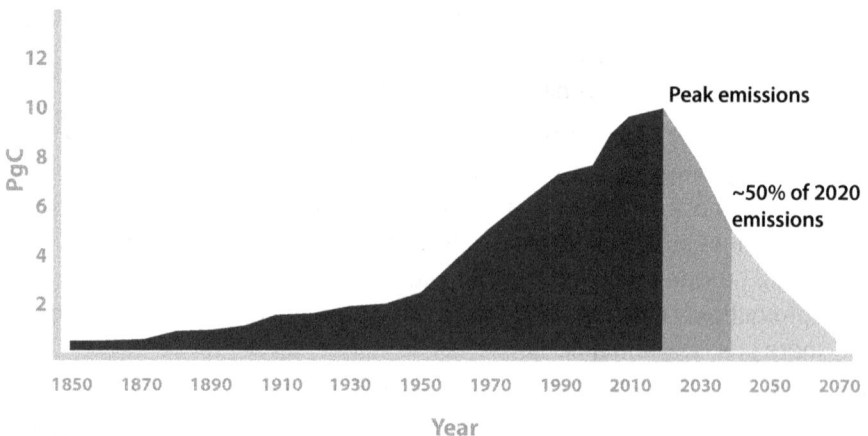

Figure 14 – UN cumulative emissions curve[clx]

Clearly, against the backdrop of continuing population growth till at least 2050, and a societal expectation of improving material standards of living, this will be no easy task. Massive scale transformations of energy, transport, energy efficiency, land use, concrete, steel and other industrial sectors will be required. Accordingly, it is critical that businesses focus on their overall (or absolute) emissions reduction.

It's generally easy to make reductions per unit of revenue or number of widgets produced. This process decreases emissions intensity. But if the revenue figure or number of widgets continues to rise, then overall those relative emissions reductions may translate into absolute emissions increases.

So what is an appropriate level of corporate emissions reduction per annum in absolute terms in the mid 2010s?

Realistically, anything much less than five percent per annum on a straight line basis is not going to be seen as pulling one's weight in the next decade or two. Depending on your organisation's starting point, however, it is not unusual to be able to yield double digit percentage decreases at low or negative cost (once energy, water and waste efficiency savings are factored) in the early stages of a corporate abatement or mitigation program.

MACs

Chapter 4 touched on a variety of ways organisations and individuals are reducing their carbon emissions. In fact there are so many ways it is often difficult to know where to start. In seeking opportunities to reduce its environmental impact, a good way to prioritise action is to develop a marginal abatement cost curve, or MAC. An example is provided in Figure 15.

Basically, a MAC takes a range of costed projects to reduce emissions (or another dimension of an organisation's environmental impact, such as water consumption) and ranks them by cost on a graph from least to highest per unit of environmental impact. The width of each bar is proportional to the amount of emissions reduction or other environmental impact abatement that is expected to be achieved. The height is the expected cost per unit of abatement.

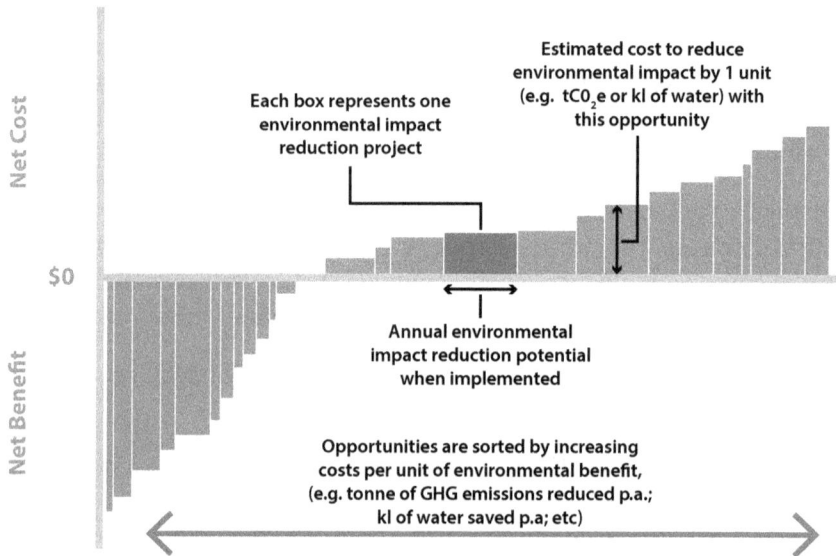

Figure 15 – Marginal abatement curve example

MACs are popular tools since they often help identify low hanging fruit: initiatives that yield environmental benefits that actually save money over the life of the project. These generally involve energy and water efficiency projects: use less energy or water and you pay lower utility bills and incidentally reduce your environmental impact. Where waste disposal (or emission) is charged by weight or volume (by governments or rubbish tips), reducing waste or improving recycling rates also delivers cost savings. If the initiative delivers a positive net present value (NPV) over the project life (or a short enough payback period), then you're in the money.

In some states or countries, government financial incentives, or the ability for a project to generate carbon credits that can then be sold, may also improve the NPV.

Above the zero line on the curve, projects rely on the organisation making a conscious decision to shoulder the cost of initiatives that deliver environmental benefits but do not yield a positive return on investment in financial accounting terms. In some cases it may be appropriate to assume a future carbon price or the imposition of charges for other environmental externalities in order to justify such initiatives. In other cases, it may be possible to base a business case on goodwill or competitive advantage that might flow, particularly given the assumption of changes in consumer sentiment.

It is worthwhile evaluating projects across separate MACs covering greenhouse emissions, water, waste and other forms of environmental impact, since particular projects may deliver benefits in several areas and in aggregate pay for themselves.

MACs should assess projects relevant to both the organisation's operational environmental impacts; those of its upstream supply chain; and of course impacts associated with the downstream use or consumption of its products and services.

Environmental abatement or mitigation projects may also become more economically feasible when they are implemented in conjunction with broader strategic or operational projects, including premises refits or relocations; plant upgrades; transitions to new products; etc.

Table 6 highlights a brief selection of potential initiatives and projects that may help reduce an organisation's environmental impact. There are many others.

Category	Suggested initiatives
Buildings & facilities	• Monitoring and maintenance (house keeping) to improve efficiency and/or reduce waste • Staff engagement and behavioural change (e.g. changing HVAC set points) • Active use of "green leases" (i.e. specific lease agreement clauses between landlord and tenant to enforce minimum efficiency and environmental impact standards) • Use of sustainable design and construction standards and materials for retrofits or new buildings
Manufacturing & service provision	• Monitoring and maintenance of plant • Staff engagement and behavioural or process change • Upgrades to improve plant efficiency • Fuel switching (to fuels with lower greenhouse gas emissions intensity) • Similarly, changes to refrigerants or other gases used in production • Product redesign to improve the efficiency of the product in use or reduce embodied energy / water / waste / pollution • Process redesign to improve the efficiency of producing a product or service, and/or to reduce embodied energy / water / waste • Use of recycled materials including shop waste
Information & communications technology (ICT)	• General house keeping (e.g. turning off equipment that is performing no useful function; consolidating workload onto fewer servers; rationalising data storage; etc.) • Use of more energy and/or water efficient data centre facilities. • Selection of ICT hardware with lower environmental impact (e.g. lower energy consumption; greater use of recycled materials; etc.) • Specific selection or development of more efficient computer software applications, which require fewer computing resources to perform equivalent functionality and/or reduce bloat-ware (inefficiency caused by unnecessary functionality) • Extend life of ICT equipment by deferring upgrade / refresh cycles. For example, desktop virtualisation technologies can prolong the useful life of user equipment
Logistics	• More efficient packaging, including reduction in materials, bulk or weight • Use of packaging with lower emissions intensity; use of recycled packaging materials • More efficiency logistics vehicles and methods • Optimisation of delivery routes • Switching to less emissions intensive and/or polluting fuels
Upstream supply chain	• Actively assess suppliers' environmental impacts and switch to lower impact providers where possible • Ensure direct suppliers understand the environmental impacts of their upstream supply chains • Ensure your organisation can trace the source of origin of raw materials used in the production of products/services • Work with suppliers to increase the use of recycled materials and in general reduce environmental impact
Downstream supply chain	• Introduce initiatives to reduce the downstream environmental impacts of the organisation's products or services • Actively engage with users of your products or services to encourage their most efficient, environmentally sensitive and long-term use • Design products to avoid "planned obsolescence" and allow prolonged use of the product with minimal need to upgrade or replace

Table 6 – Sample environmental impact reduction opportunities

Chapter 13
Risk and Resilience

Part 1 introduced models for assessing the risks of a changing climate to a given organisation. Recapping briefly, the key dimensions to consider, as repeated in Figure 16 included the organisation's:

- Strategic impacts – the intensity of its operations in terms of greenhouse gas emissions and other environmental degradation
- Operational resilience – its exposure to the first and second order impacts of climate change

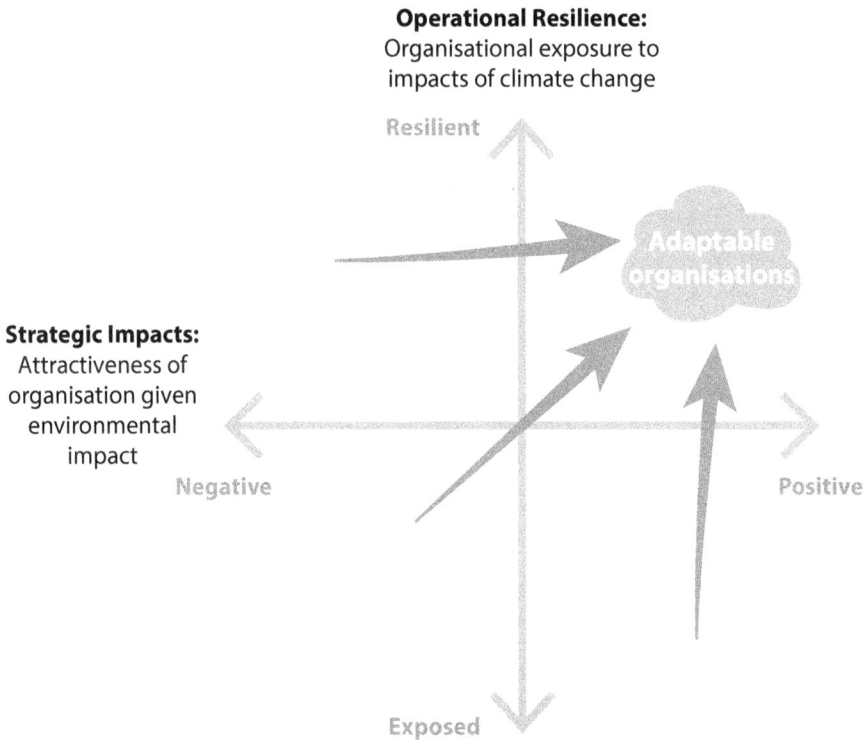

Operational Resilience:
Organisational exposure to impacts of climate change

Resilient

Adaptable organisations

Strategic Impacts:
Attractiveness of organisation given environmental impact

Negative

Positive

Exposed

Figure 16: Key dimensions of organisational climate risk

Organisations that have lumped climate considerations within a broader operational risk management review may be missing both societal or structural changes that may impact on their industry or the potential upside that comes when it is considered as a potential strategic business opportunity.

To determine an organisation's position on the impacts / resilience scale it is necessary to undertake a more detailed risk assessment to identify individual threats and plot each of them on the traditional probability / impact matrix. This involves taking a systems thinking approach to the business, its assets, up- and down-stream supply chain and its relationship with the external environment, as shown in Figure 17.

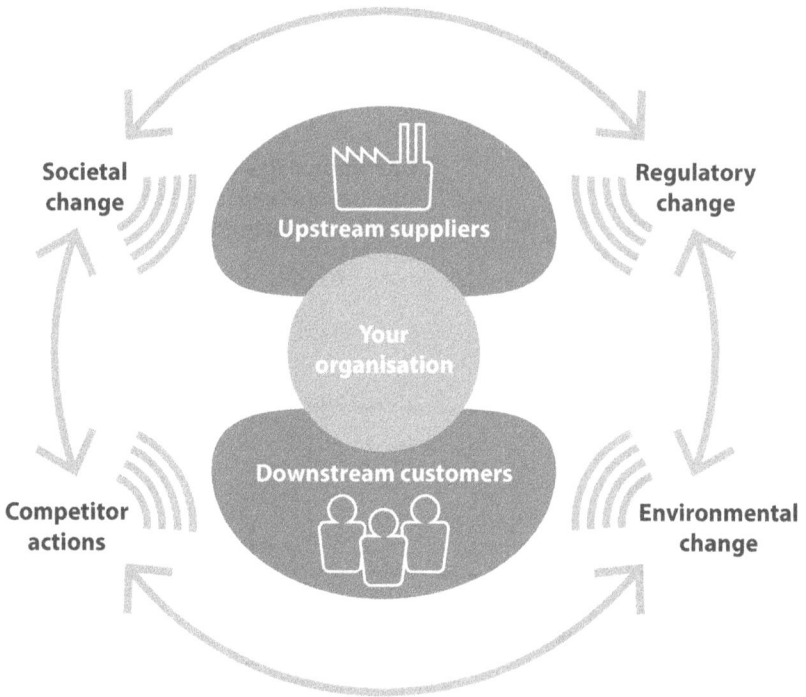

Figure 17: System wide risk assessment

Table 7 highlights a sample of threats that an organisation could be exposed to, which can be used as a point of departure:

Category	Underlying Threat	Effects on Organisation	Consequences
Physical / Operational	• Increasing average temps • Changing rainfall patterns • Increasing frequency / intensity of extreme weather (storms, flooding / inundation, lightning, bushfire, heat waves, drought, etc.) • Disease vectors • Sea level rise • Ocean degradation	• Damage/loss of assets (buildings, plant, people, agricultural productivity, etc.) • Inability to conduct business • Impaired service provision from utilities, suppliers, etc. • Reduced demand for the organisation's products/services (if customers are also impacted or product is less needed given changed physical conditions)	• Increased costs (some may not be covered by insurance) • Reputation damage (if organisation cannot service clients) • Reduced revenue (short term if operation is impaired; longer term due to reputation damage) • Legal / regulatory action (e.g. if operating conditions breached by impairment) • Insolvency if impacts are significant and prolonged
Reputation / Regulatory	• Consumer revolt against highly-polluting / degrading industries • Carbon & other pollution taxes • Loss of subsidies • Regulations tightened to limit polluting / degrading activities • Class action law suits	• Increasing input costs • Customer defection • Loss of "license to operate" • Reduced access to capital markets • Fines / sanctions	• Declining margins • Reduced revenue • Reduced valuation • Increasing cost of capital • Insolvency • Forced closure
Strategic / Structural	• Decline of underlying natural asset such as snow, coral reef, beach, forest, pollinators, fish stocks, etc. • Declining viability of coastal property / infrastructure assets • Increasing costs for food, water, insurance, etc. (due to exposure to physical impacts) • Increasing taxes as governments struggle to raise revenue to prop up failing infrastructure	• Reduced viability of product or reduced productivity due to decline of natural asset • Additional costs to maintain quality of natural asset as it declines • Costs to protect viability of property / infrastructure assets • Fewer customers • Fewer buyers for exposed assets	• Loss of revenue as demand declines • Declining margins as costs increase • Reduced valuation • Insolvency

Table 7 – Threats and consequences

From this broad set of considerations specific risks can be identified and categorised. Risks should be expressed in the syntax of an "if/then" statement, i.e. "if [particular threat or hazard] occurs and affects [particular aspect of the organisation, its operations, supply chain partners, etc.], then [consequence, expressed in terms of specific impacts including financial, reputational, regulatory, etc.]".

The organisation's vulnerability will depend on its sensitivity to the threat, the particular controls it already has in place to deal with this or similar threats, and the effectiveness of such controls. Effective controls may offset the risk of a particular threat by either reducing the probability of it affecting the organisation, or by reducing the impact if it does occur.

Given that climate change marks a departure from the status quo, it is important to think about potential tipping points that could cause new risks, or cause existing risks to become more material. This then leads to a list of risks that has a temporal aspect to it: risks are either present today, or at some point in the future are expected to appear or may become significantly more intense. If the organisation relies on long term capital assets (and particularly if such assets are relatively illiquid or could become so), it is important to forecast how key risks might emerge or change in five, 10 or even 30 years' time.

This is highlighted in Table 8.

A business impact analysis (BIA) can be undertaken to assess how the loss or impairment of each part of the business' system (be it a particular supplier, system, property, port, person or whatever) would affect the organisation's finances, reputation, legal and regulatory compliance and so on. The impact of a range of external cost or demand shocks such as the imposition of carbon taxes or other regulatory change, competitor actions, changing societal attitudes (and the way these interact with each other) also need to be taken into account. Exposure is highly specific to the organisation, its activities, operational and market geographies, jurisdictions and timeframe.

Positioning of particular risks along the likelihood and consequences axes of the risk matrix may require input from engineering, meteorological, legal and other specialists as well as internal disciplines. The scale for the probability and impact axes should be defined in terms that are appropriate for the organisation in question. A catastrophic financial impact for a small organisation could be insignificant for a larger business.

At this point it is possible to assign a specific risk rating to each identified risk. If a tipping point is associated with a risk, then an alternate combination of probability and impact can be allocated as shown in Table 9 and the resulting risk levels plotted on the matrix (Figure 10).

With a good understanding of your climate and environmental risk exposures, the next step is to develop treatment strategies to reduce each of the risks. There are four major treatment options and they are often implemented in combination:

- Accept the risk and do nothing. This may be a perfectly valid strategy in the case of minor risks, or those that are subject to a tipping point that is expected to be a number of years away;

- Avoid the risk by taking steps to reduce the probability of its occurrence (moving the risk down the vertical scale on the matrix);

- Reduce the impact of the risk if it does occur (moving the risk left along the horizontal scale); or

- Transfer the risk to a third party. However, traditional risk transfer mechanisms such as insurance or risk financing may be unavailable for high probability events or could become increasingly expensive over time as probabilities increase. Critically, risk transfer can generally only cover financial impacts and does not deal effectively with damage to an organisation's reputation.

Ref	Risk Description	Existing Controls	Effectiveness of Existing Controls	Is Risk Subject to a Tipping Point?	Timing of Tipping Point	Impact on Risk Level
Rx	E.g. If [hazard] affects [aspect of operation] then [consequence] Impacts could accrue to: • Particular product / service / brand • Operational process • Assets / buildings / etc. • Underlying natural assets • Logistics • Direct suppliers • Upstream logistics • Downstream logistics • Customers / consumers • Competitors	• Business continuity / disaster recovery arrangements • Crisis management plans • Insurance • Supplier diversity • Operational diversity • Breadth of product/service portfolio • Customer / market diversity • Contractual relief • Lobbying (company / industry) • Etc.	• High • Medium • Low	E.g.: • Major global agreement on carbon pricing • Confluence of events attributed to climate change influences consumer / political sentiment • Change of government • Disruptive competitor action / emergence of substitute • Etc.	• Unknown • <1 year • 2-5 years • 6+ years	• Improves • Neutral • Minor Decrease • Significant decrease
R1	If a major coastal storm surge at [location] leads to inundation of [facility], then each incident is estimated to cause stock and facility damage in the order of $[x] million and operational outages of 1-4 weeks. Currently the estimated frequency of such evens is 1 in 20 years	Business continuity plans have limited effectiveness as this is the only regional facility capable of providing this function. Insurance covers about 90% of direct losses but premiums are increasing and the loss of customer goodwill is not covered. Supply contracts contain standard force majeure clauses that are applicable for this type of event, but as the likelihood increases it is expected that customers will seek alternate remedies.	• Medium	If sea levels rise by 20cm or more (the same amount as has occurred over the last century) then major storm surges at [location] will be magnified by a factor of y%. In this case [facility] is expected to be subject to inundation 2-3 times per annum. Potential collapse of significant ice sheets could dramatically accelerate the current rate of sea level rise	• 6+ years	• Significant decrease
⋮						
Rn						

Table 8 – Risks and tipping points

Ref	Current Timeframe				Future Timeframe (e.g. if tipping point reached) (Rx')			
	Probability	Impact	Risk Level	Treatment Approach	Probability	Impact	Risk Level	Treatment Approach
Rx	Rare Unlikely Moderate Likely Almost certain	Insignificant Minor Moderate Major Catastrophic	Minor Moderate Significant Severe	Accept Avoid Reduce Transfer	Rare Unlikely Moderate Likely Almost certain	Insignificant Minor Moderate Major Catastrophic	Minor Moderate Significant Severe	Accept Avoid Reduce Transfer
R1	Unlikely	Minor	Significant	Transfer	Likely	Major	Severe	Avoid
...								
Rn								

Table 9 – Risk ratings: current and future

Probability of occurance (in a given time frame)	Impact of occurence				
	Insignificant	Minor	Moderate	Major	Catastrophic
Almost Certain					
Likely				R1′	
Moderate					
Unlikely				R1	
Rare					

Figure 18 – Risk matrix: with future tipping point adjustments

In developing resilience through effective risk management, one of the key requirements of any risk treatment is that its costs within a given period must be less than the expected loss (probability x financial impact) should the hazard occur.

In practice, this is easier said than done given the difficulty of attributing probabilities and accurately assessing the impacts of uncertain and generally infrequent events. Another factor that will determine the selected risk treatment option(s) for a given risk is the organisation's specific risk appetite, which is often heavily influenced by the culture of the senior leadership team.

For each risk, specific treatment options can now be identified and assessed. Given the broad nature but relatively gradual onset of some climate related risks it is appropriate to develop a risk treatment roadmap: an integrated program of initiatives to be implemented in sequence over a multi-year period. Timing-wise, initiatives are prioritised by a combination of cost effectiveness versus the proximity of the threat (i.e. whether the threat is current or is not a consideration unless/until a particular tipping point is reached).

Initiatives requiring extensive capital expenditure or disruption are often scheduled around depreciation cycles, property leases or other triggers that help catalyse the business case for action. A framework for assessing options is provided in Table 10.

Ref	Option Ref	Specific Treatment Options	Timing / Triggers	Cost	Effectiveness	Option Priority

Rx	Ox	**Physical Vulnerability**
		• Upgrade facilities or relocate / duplicate
		• Improve supply chain & logistics resilience
		• Ensure resilience for critical infrastructure providers
		• Ensure effective business continuity management & insurance cover
		Reputation / Regulatory Vulnerability
		• Reduce environmental impact
		  • Direct operations
		  • Supply chain
		  • Products/services
		  • Environmental certifications
		• Divest from polluting businesses / products
		• If possible exploit core competencies while transitioning to non-polluting industries / products
		Industry / Structural Vulnerability
		• Relocate operation to area that is less exposed or will benefit from future climate change
		• Consider technological change or product adaptation
		• Divest early to minimise loss of value
		• Consider sale of asset but reatining the operation as interim step
			ASAP or, for example, in conjunction with:
			• Product model lifecycles
			• Depreciation / CapEx cycles
			• Lease expiries
				Relative to the organisation's overall budget:
				• High
				• Medium
				• Low
					Assess residual risk level (probability x impact) if implemented:
					• Very high: (decrease risk three levels e.g. Severe to Minor)
					• High: (two level decrease e.g. Severe to Moderate)
					• Medium: (one level decrease)
					• Low: (no change to risk level)
						Order by relative effectiveness @ lowest cost
						• High
						• Medium
						• Low

R1	O1	Implement a flood barrier at [facility] at driveway entrance to basement. This would reduce inundation damage significantly by protecting basement electrical plant.	ASAP	Low	Medium	Medium
R1'	O2	Relocate processing facility away from coast	Lease expiry (2017); Plant depreciation (2019)	High	Very high	High
...	...					
Rx	On					

Table 10 – Risk treatment assessment

Organisations with long term capital assets or exposures should plan further ahead and anticipate several "waves" of risk mitigation / adaptation as risk profile changes as highlighted in Figure 19.

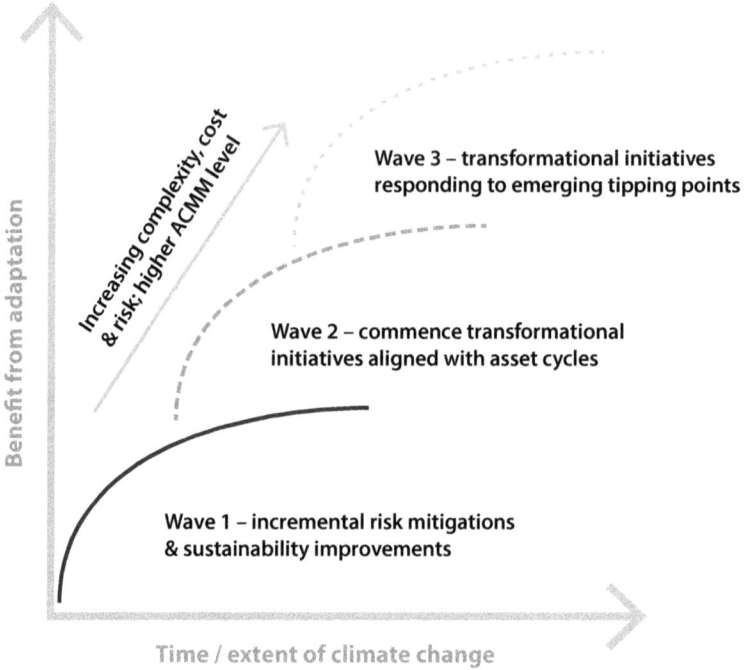

Figure 19 – Staged risk mitigation over time as risk increases

Finally, this can be developed into a costed risk treatment action register (Table 11). In particular, this highlights the extent to which each risk is expected to be reduced or avoided as a result of implementing the various initiatives, so that the residual risk level can be understood. Ideally, all risks can be reduced to a minor level and the residual risk then accepted (Figure 20).

Probability of occurance (in a given time frame)	Impact of occurence				
	Insignificant	Minor	Moderate	Major	Catastrophic
Almost Certain					
Likely				R1'	
Moderate					
Unlikely			R1+O1 (A1)	R1	
Rare	R1'+O2 (A2)				

Figure 20 – Risk matrix: with treatment options applied

Action	Risk Ref	Level	Treatment Option	Description	Residual Probability	Residual Impact	Residual Risk Level	Priority	Timing	Cost	Status
Ax	Rx	Minor Moderate Significant Severe	Ox	[From Table 10]	Rare Unlikely Moderate Likely Almost certain	Insignificant Minor Moderate Major Catastrophic	Minor Moderate Significant Severe	High Medium Low	E.g. specific year or quarter	$	Planning Pending Approved Rejected
A1	R1	Significant	O1	Severe weather upgrade to processing facility	Unlikely	Moderate	Moderate	Medium	Q2 2016	$250k	Approved
A2	R1'	Severe	O2	Relocate processing facility away from flood plain	Rare	Insignificant	Minor	Very high	2019 (assuming lease can be extended to align with plant depreciation)	$10m	Pending

Table 11 – Risk treatment action register

Practitioners will realise that the process outlined above is basically a nuanced version of a standard risk assessment and risk treatment process detailed within the ISO 31000 standard for Risk Management.

The key take away from this chapter is the need to look beyond so-called "business as usual" risks and examine the broader climatic and attitudinal shifts that are playing out at a more subtle level over a longer time frame, plus the tipping points that may precipitate discontinuous changes in business conditions.

Of course, risk is not necessarily all about down-side. An effective risk management process also seeks to identify opportunities – the proverbial cloud with a silver lining – such as the ideas contained within Part 2 of this book.

Once the risks are understood the challenge is to implement the treatment measures to make the organisation more resilient. The resilience strategy for a business includes **operational**, **cultural** and **strategic** elements as highlighted in Figure 21.

At an **operational** level, resilience is about:

- preventing events that could interrupt business operations;
- preparedness measures to reduce the risks if such events do occur, including;
- response mechanisms to limit damage or disruption; and
- recovery processes, systems, facilities, etc. to help the organisation get back to normal as quickly as possible.

Operational resilience is important because when sudden events occur (including natural disasters and those with human-causes such as operational failures, acts of terrorism or sabotage, fires, information technology shut downs, etc.), some organisations will suffer minimal consequences, while a considerable proportion that are less prepared fail to recover to the same level or commence a downward revenue spiral due to the damage the incident has done to their reputations.

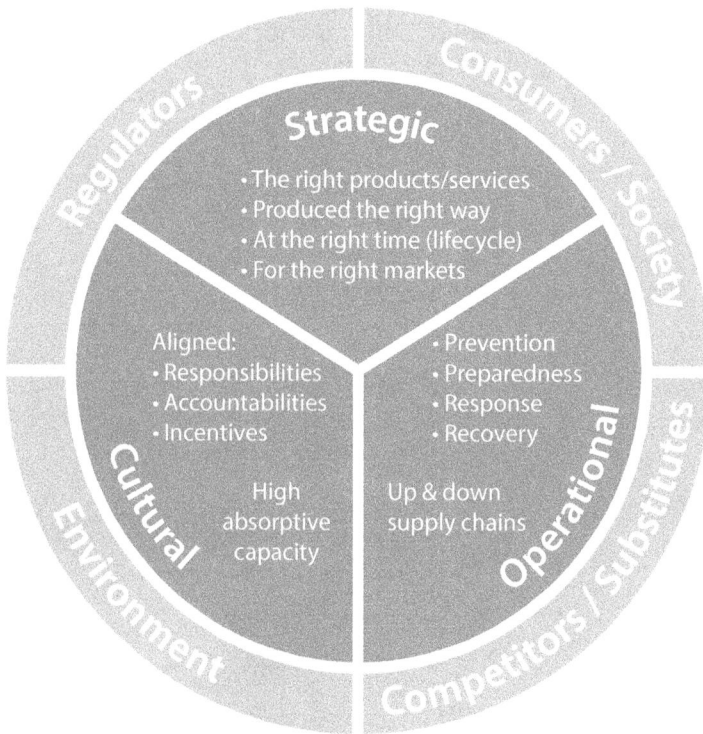

Figure 21 – Components of Business Resilience

All social groups develop a unique **culture** of shared history, ideas and behavioural norms, which in turn shape their responses to events. At a cultural level, resilient companies have clearly defined values, responsibilities and accountabilities and appropriately aligned incentives that help them make the right decisions to adapt and thrive as conditions change. While strong leadership can help shape an organisation's culture, some elements may be deeply entrenched within large bureaucracies and are very difficult to change.

As we saw in an earlier chapter, an organisation's Absorptive Capacity is a key product of its organisational culture. For example, businesses with a traditional hierarchical command and control ethos are potentially less likely to appreciate vulnerabilities or changes in their environment that may threaten their operation. Businesses used to dynamic change and which adopt a more meritocratic approach may be more likely to be constantly evaluating the risks and opportunities to their business and establishing robust resilience.

The **strategic** aspect to resilience is about providing the right products/ services in the right way at the right time (in terms of the product/service lifecycle) to the right markets, which is the main focus of the next chapter.

Chapter 14
Adaptive Strategy

In the last quarter of the 20th century, photographic film giant Eastman Kodak dominated a photography eco-system, with a range of high margin film, chemical and print consumables, plus low cost basic cameras covering the needs of holiday snappers through to professionals. Today Kodak is a shadow of its former self and focuses on business imaging solutions, having emerged from Chapter 11 bankruptcy in 2013.

It's no secret that Kodak failed to transform itself effectively in response to the disruptive threat/opportunity of digital photography. The subsequent shift saw many people cease physically printing their images, relying instead on recording their life history on Facebook and other social media, and viewing their images on laptops, tablets or phones.

Kodak, despite being the inventors of the first digital camera in 1975 and in the mid 2000s the dominant manufacturer of digital cameras to the U.S. market, are not the only corporate casualty of that market disruption. In 2006, for example, Konica Minolta announced it was ceasing film and camera production after 78 years. Even Kodak's major rival Fujifilm is now a relative minnow of the consumer digital photography world though it too has carved a niche for itself in business optical and imaging products.

Meanwhile, the consumer products of long standing analogue camera makers Nikon and Canon, both of whom adapted reasonably well to the digital photography revolution, have been largely displaced by cameras built into smart phones.

Indeed, it's instructive to review the list of companies that have been around for more than 100 years or so. Many have undergone a number of transformations and the products or services they relied on in their early history are sometimes completely different from those they are known for today.

Take computing giant IBM, for example, whose origins date back to the 1880s and was born out of a holding company whose subsidiaries produced the ubiquitous Bundy clocks favoured by time conscious employers, plus "weighing scales, automatic meat slicers [and] coffee grinders" amongst others. The International Business Machines name was coined in 1924 and the company specialised in adding machines and electric typewriters before developing true computer systems in the post-World War 2 period. In the early 1990s the company faced near bankruptcy after failing to anticipate the change from mainframe to personal computers. Today, the company remains a behemoth due to its decision to move into services-based businesses, which now contribute well over half its revenues.[clxi]

Many other venerable companies' present revenue streams bear little resemblance to the products that originally made them great. General Electric's 1880s origins as Thomas Edison's agglomeration of several lighting and electrical generation companies is a far cry from today's global giant with diversified interest in aviation, finance, healthcare, energy, water and transportation.

Companies ignore or fight disruption at their peril: the most successful are those that are adept at adaptation.

The corporate history of the digital photography disruption provides a great example of the types of company-destroying change that could be brought about by the Adaptive Economy. For example, one such disruption is currently playing out in the energy utilities sector.

Energy utilities typically comprise the following components:

- generation (power stations or wells in the case of gas);
- transmission & distribution (the so-called "poles and wires" or network, gas pipelines, etc.); and
- retail (buys energy on the wholesale market and sells it to residential and business consumers).

While there is often a level of competition feasible at the generation and retail end, the network component is a natural monopoly given the significant capital investment required. As such, companies in this space have traditionally been very profitable, often despite (or because of) government regulation.

In Chapter 4 we saw how roof-top solar and other local schemes are leading to energy efficiencies and emissions reduction. However, this disaggregation of electricity generation is causing increasing headaches for established energy utilities, particularly in the network space, who are finding their traditional business model is under threat, particularly if customers choose to go fully "off grid".

Transmission and distribution providers' cost bases are predominantly fixed, so the same expenses need to be shared amongst a declining number of customers, which increases the marginal network charges that are passed onto individual consumers. Each cost increase makes the business case more compelling for consumers to switch to rooftop solar and batteries or some other means of local generation, particularly as increasing economies of scale and technological innovation are driving down the costs of going off grid. And so the spiral of decline continues.

There are potential reliability issues associated with becoming your own electricity generator and not everybody is willing to take on the challenge. As such, innovative companies (including some of the energy retailers) are jumping on the bandwagon to provide "build, own, operate" models enabling consumers to enjoy many of the benefits of going off grid but without some of the risks. Some are providing financing arrangements where customers can avoid the upfront costs and simply pay a per kilowatt hour rate. And others are starting to experiment with micro-grids, pooling local generation and storage at a neighbourhood level and providing low or no carbon emissions generation combined with low transmission losses plus the added benefits of improved system resilience and specialist maintenance.

Simultaneously, the upstream industry (large scale remote generators in addition to network providers) has lobbied governments to complicate or frustrate plans for micro-grids, creating bureaucratic obstacles on safety and other grounds with some valid concerns but an underlying motivation to protect their market dominance. Are they fighting a rear guard action? Time will tell.

While a subset of organisations will capitalise on the various emerging products and services introduced in Part 2, many will continue to produce a similar range of goods and services to those they do today.

In the Adaptive Economy, however, we think leading companies will be distinguished by their ability to produce:

- The right products or services. By this we mean things that fulfill a viable and environmentally acceptable customer need;

- In the right way. In other words, using production methods and sourcing materials that demonstrably have the least environmental impact compared to alternatives, and ideally have a net positive environmental benefit;

- At the right time. There's no point continuing to make products or services when demand for them is declining, particularly if that decrease is caused by customers switching to more environmentally acceptable substitutes or alternatives;

- For the right markets. Again, if the market for your goods or services is being undermined by a changing climate, then you may be on a downward trend.

Of course, often a company's strategy will be influenced by a variety of drivers for change, and environmental considerations may be secondary to other factors.

Let's take an example of an industry that initially seems to have very little connection with climate change: information management. A number of companies provide services to warehouse documents and computer backup tapes on behalf of business customers. Their business model involves real estate costs for the storage facilities, but typically the bulk of their revenue comes from logistics: collection and delivery of paper records or tapes.

This type of business is undesirable from an environmental perspective for several reasons:

- Use of paper records is materials intensive. Depending on the source of the paper, it may have contributed to deforestation; paper production is water intensive and leads to chemical waste given the bleaches and other chemicals used to achieve the grades of paper required by laser printers. Even recycled paper is relatively energy and water intensive. Office printers are also resource intensive, particularly in terms of the various consumables they require. In Australia alone it has been estimated that over 18 million toner cartridges are disposed of annually, producing 5,000 tonnes of waste.[clxii] Again the associated chemicals cause environmental damage as they leach into the soil and ground water.

- Physically moving paper (or backup tapes) around is energy intensive. Paper is heavy and relatively bulky. It takes a fair amount of fuel to move a truck full of file boxes.

- Even storing paper is not very environmentally sensitive: land is used for the warehouse; there is embodied energy and other environmental degradation inherent in the building's materials and construction; and in most climates the facility must have a level of climate control to prevent deterioration of the documents over time (for example from mould in humid environments). This means there needs to be some sort of air conditioning system, which again uses energy.

Many services-based businesses, as part of their sustainability programs, are claiming initiatives that reduce paper consumption. It follows, perhaps, that sustainability considerations might be a significant driver in the decline of the information management business. But in reality, two stronger forces are driving change in the sector:

- Changing use of technology (accelerated by generational change in the workforce), which is making paper records increasingly obsolete; and
- The inclusion of electronic records as a valid form of evidence in legal matters.

Increasingly, records and correspondence are created in electronic form. If they are printed, it is either because the recipient prefers a hardcopy to read/annotate; or because a hand-written signature is required. In either case, the document can then be scanned and indexed, and becomes a digital record. There is little need to maintain the hardcopy original, since the digital version is generally admissible as evidence should it be required for legal purposes.

Meanwhile, the need to send computer backup tapes off-site is also in decline, driven by factors such as the decreasing cost of disk-based storage and network bandwidth, coupled with the rise of distributed, cloud-based data centres. It is now affordable for many businesses to back up their data "over the wire" (using a network link) to a storage array at a remote data centre. Rather than maintaining a hierarchy of daily, weekly and monthly backups and shuffling tapes between the main site and offsite storage facilities, data snapshots are made directly onto the remote disk drives. Indeed, many businesses now synchronise their data between two (or more) data centres in real time.

So, while sustainability considerations (reduced paper, reduced Scope 3 greenhouse gas emissions) may influence some business' move to reduce their use of traditional information management firms; in most cases it will be driven by cost savings and productivity benefits afforded by technology and relaxed evidentiary standards. Nevertheless, the traditional information management sector in aggregate is on a slow decline, and may be obsolete within a couple of decades.

How are the firms in the sector responding? One approach has been to introduce document imaging services, to help organisations digitise their paper records. This approach is likely to generate revenue that may offset the decline of the core business. However, in a world where a majority of records are now being created and stored digitally, imaging offers at best a temporary reprieve. Once paper originals that are not already stored in a content management system have been archived (or once their retention periods are reached – in most cases less than 10 years) there is no longer a requirement to image them.

Some information management firms are attempting to position themselves as the provider of on-line content management and workflow systems. This approach may provide longer-term benefits. However, just because they are good with storing, shifting and retrieving physical records, doesn't necessarily translate to expertise in information technology systems. At a minimum, it requires a significantly different set of skills and a major transformation from such firms' traditional focus on logistics and real estate.

And what of the real estate portfolio, which becomes redundant as the physical storage demand declines? If the business leases the warehouse space then it can consolidate over time (though below a certain warehouse size the costs of storage will become uncompetitive). For those that own their sites, the challenge is to spin it off while it can still fetch a good price, as one prominent US-based provider has done by securitising its warehouse portfolio, effectively turning itself into a real estate investment trust.

The conclusion from this example is that while environmental factors may not be a dominant factor in transforming an industry, they can be a catalyst. And it is worthwhile examining which directions the catalyst of climate change and other environmental issues might take an industry, since it may also help identify other disruptions that might affect technology developments, customer and competitor actions.

In the next few sections we'll break down the four strategic criteria exhibited by leading companies in the Adaptive Economy.

The right products and services

By this we mean things that fulfill a viable and environmentally acceptable customer need. Viability of customer need is relatively simple: it means you're producing a good or service for which enough customers are prepared to pay you a price that means you can turn a profit. But what about the environmentally acceptable aspect?

There are plenty of products and services that fulfill a viable market need but are anything but environmentally acceptable. Destroying sensitive wildlife habitat to build a retirement village on the edge of an attractive lake is a great example: there are plenty of people who'd like to live close to nature in their old age, but that doesn't mean it's an ethically appropriate thing to do.

Just because coal is an efficient, convenient and relatively inexpensive source of energy doesn't mean it is the right product to use (or, if you're a bank, an appropriate investment to lend to). For one thing, it causes billions of dollars of public health costs from the associated respiratory conditions its consumption causes, notwithstanding its contribution to global warming.

Nor are furniture, paper or building products sourced from unsustainably harvested forests appropriate products in the Adaptive Economy, or products that use virgin materials when recycled alternatives are available (or would rapidly become cost effective if more organisations sourced them). Or how about commercial scale fishing operations that deplete fisheries stocks and lead to massive by-catch? Producing something using a low cost method with economies of scale does not imply sustainability.

Engineers that fail to incorporate high standards of energy or water efficiency into their designs; accountants (and their professional associations) whose advice fails to help businesses appreciate the costs of their environmental externalities (even on a shadow price basis); even services organisations whose environmental footprint is generally seen as relatively neutral can influence better environmental outcomes.

Producing environmentally acceptable products and services needn't cost more, particularly once economies of scale and "mainstreaming" of environmentally sustainable design principles is achieved. For example, these days there is little, if any, premium for sourcing building materials that offer significantly reduced environmental impacts (in manufacture and/or operation) compared with traditional alternatives. It may take a little longer to assess the relative environmental merits of competing products (and the impacts of incorporating them into the particular building project), but there is a growing body of evidence to suggest that so-called "green" buildings are quicker to lease and may attract a valuation premium.[clxiii]

Produced the right way

Organisations should examine every part of the value chain of their products or services to ensure they are treading as lightly as they possibly can. From materials to production processes to the design of the item to distribution and of course use or consumption and end of life treatment, there are generally hundreds of ways that the environmental impact of products and services can be reduced. The first step on this journey, as has been articulated earlier, is to undertake a Life Cycle Assessment (LCA). This can be compared with competitors and substitutes to identify whether it is a relative asset or liability.

We are already seeing a growing minority of consumers (both personal and corporate) becoming more discerning about the environmental impact of their purchases, and this trend is likely to increase. The ability of a company to provide impartial and unvarnished data about the impacts of its offerings is an important first step; converting that to a competitive advantage involves an understanding of competitors' LCAs and, depending on that data, a willingness to re-engineer products and processes to improve environmental outcomes.

It is expected that within the next decade, some governments will agree on standards for LCA methodologies for a variety of product categories and will legislate or regulate to require such data to be displayed in advertising and at point of sale. For example, this could extend the current energy and water efficiency labeling on appliances to consider a range of environmental impacts associated with materials extraction, processing, manufacturing and transportation, plus of course the arrangements for end of life disposal / recycling.

Even without a full LCA, it is generally possible to identify inefficiencies and other environmentally damaging practices. Often, the cost of improving these can be offset through savings in materials, energy, water or waste disposal costs. As discussed in Chapter 12, use of the Marginal Abatement Curve methodology can assist with these processes. However, bear in mind that measures that might improve, say, manufacturing efficiency could potentially result in more adverse consequences elsewhere in the value chain, which is why undertaking a Life Cycle Assessment is so important.

In time, we expect leading organisations will:

- Avoid the exploitation of depleted or vulnerable natural assets;
- Use materials recovered from recycled goods or materials, creating closed loop systems;
- Source renewable, non-polluting energy;
- Use materials, energy and water in an efficient and sustainable way;
- Produce non-toxic products, or if they are toxic (to people or the environment) they will be produced and used in such a way that the toxicity is contained;
- Not pollute the environment at any stage of their supply chain or lifecycle;
- Minimise packaging waste;
- Design products that are durable (able to be used many times over an extended period); transferable (to new owners or users); and easily disassembled and recycled;
- Discourage early obsolescence and replacement of their products (such as the approach taken by active-wear brand Patagonia);
- Actively encourage government, corporate and consumer behaviours that reduce society's environmental impact; and
- Ensure their businesses and supply chains are resilient against the impacts of climate change.

At the right time

There's no point continuing to invest in products or services when demand for them is declining, particularly if that decrease is caused by customers switching to more environmentally acceptable competitors or substitutes. Virtually all products and services exhibit the type of lifecycle shown in Figure 22, featuring differing sales, costs and profitability characteristics through each of four phases. A key business challenge is to identify when mature products are in danger of decline, and to start lining up viable alternatives.

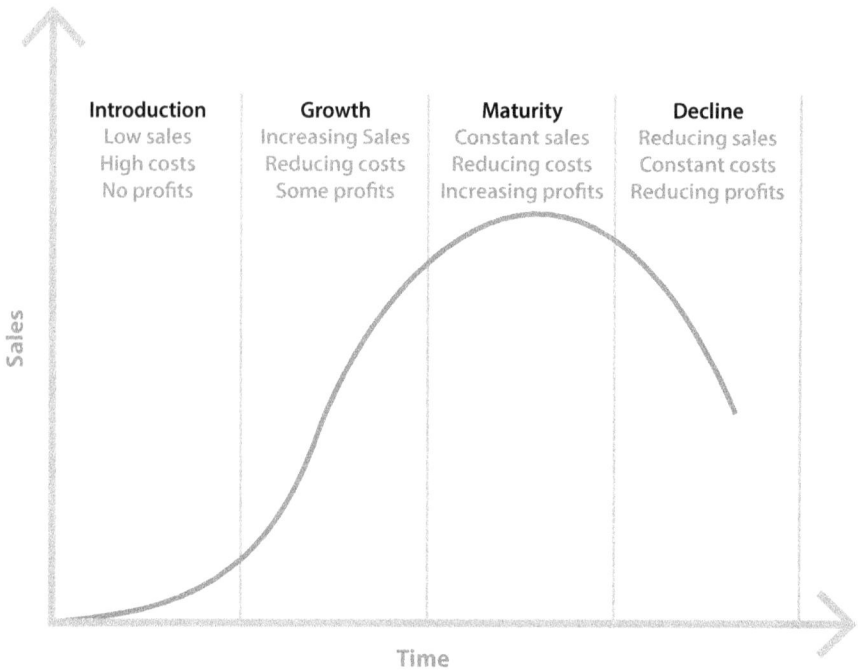

Figure 22 – Product/Service Lifecycle

Causes for declining sales could include:

- A superior offer from competitors for a similar product, typically in terms of similar quality for a reduced price point; but potentially in future due to a reduced environmental impact. An example might be beef producers that can demonstrate significantly reduced greenhouse emissions per kilogram, perhaps through the use of feed additives that reduce livestock methane emissions or a new method of trapping and sequestering such emissions.

- Declining demand for the product category, which might be due to:
  - Flagging interest in a "fad" style fashion product. The once ubiquitous 1980s Velcro wallets spring to mind. In future, particularly if governments eventually impose effective lifecycle assessment labeling requirements on products and services, the overall market for fashion goods may decline somewhat.

- The introduction of a substitute product/service (i.e. one that fulfills a similar consumer need – high speed trains versus air travel for inter-state routes, for example), which offers a superior customer experience. Again, substitutes that deliver reduced environmental impact may begin to be preferred, particularly if other characteristics and price are comparable.

- The decline of an underlying asset on which the category depends. An example might be cafes, bars or accommodation in beach-side locales if the beach is regularly eroded by severe storms.

- Regulatory changes that alter the price structure relative to substitutes: carbon taxes imposed on emissions intensive activities such as coal-fired electricity generation, for example.

- The corollary is that the price of the substitute becomes more competitive due to economies of scale as the technology matures, or access to subsidies. As seen earlier, this is occurring in many markets with regard to solar and wind generation.

Rather than exiting a market sector altogether on environmental grounds, it may be better to plug the gap that could be filled by more opportunistic businesses (including potential substitutes) by switching to more environmentally acceptable materials, production methods and/or lifecycle statistics. For example, some (but by no means all) of the oil majors are starting to look beyond fossil fuels, making significant investments in renewable energy.

For the right markets

Geographic markets for some products and services will decline over time, such as coastal tourism in areas where beaches are routinely eroded by major storms, or alpine sports in regions where the ski slopes can't move high enough up the mountain to outpace the receding snow line.

The market for other products may decline over time, as consumers become more aware of the environmental consequences. For example, even if local growing conditions for a particular fruit or vegetable are relatively unaffected by a changing climate, the transport emissions associated with its importation may deter consumers in foreign export markets from purchasing it. Already there is a niche but growing "local food" movement. This trend might be accelerated by a change of labeling standards, making embodied emissions for food more readily comparable.

Over time (and in most cases still many years off), market viability will start to take on a new and more urgent meaning: are your target segments still going to be there; is the hook upon which your business depends still going to be relevant?

In the event that we experience runaway climate change this century, then as a society we will generally move down rather than up Maslow's traditional hierarchy of needs. Rather than seeking aspirational products and services that fulfill our needs for self-esteem and self-actualization, our more pressing issues could focus around basic personal and family needs of security, health, food, water and shelter.

The road to transformation

As we saw in the preceding chapter, organisations responding to climate change (or other disruptive challenges) are likely to undergo a number of strategic metamorphoses over several decades, matching their response to changing conditions and aligning initiatives with capital and market cycles. Figure 23 summarises the various levels of opportunity that an organisation can adopt, ranging from the tactical, such as efficiency and reliability improvements to broad-scale strategic transformation.

Making big strategic plays such as transitioning out of major product lines that have a doubtful future, or into products with an unproven track record obviously involves significant risk. It is critical to bring a company's investors along on the journey, which is where the interaction with that group of stakeholders becomes critical, as touched on in Chapter 11.

Protect your brands and organisation from "climate obsolescence"

Develop new products and services:
• To reduce society's environmental impact
• To assist with adaptation to climate change impacts

Reposition your brand as a climate leader to grow market share

Overhaul processes, facilities & supply chains to yield efficiency & reliability benefits

Figure 23 – Levels of opportunity

Chapter 15
Starting Your Journey

It should be clear by now that the transition to the Adaptive Economy is going to be a challenging and fraught process. The next few decades are likely to be tumultuous as we belatedly come to the realisation that our control over nature is far from complete and very impermanent.

Recapping the major themes we have covered:

Introduction

- The global climate is changing and human activities are largely responsible. Like it or not, our dependence on fossil fuels, combined with other steps we have taken to upset the natural carbon cycle, have increased the levels of atmospheric greenhouse gases.

- This has already contributed to an increase in global average temperatures of about one degree Celsius; which is translating to a greater incidence of extreme weather events and a host of local impacts on land and in the oceans that are starting to become increasingly visible.

- Despite international efforts to achieve meaningful reduction in human greenhouse gas emissions, a variety of psychological and other factors mean it is unlikely that we will avert significant levels of global warming and associated climate change.

Part 1 – Risk

- Consequently, and compounded by increasing supply chain complexity and other factors, the risk matrix of many organisations is becoming more crowded, with new risks appearing and others increasing in probability or impact, while risk transfer mechanisms such as insurance will become less effective or affordable over time.

- All businesses potentially face adverse risks from exposure to the direct impacts of a changing climate such as damage or disruption to facilities or supply chain partners from extreme weather events. Many businesses will also face increased input costs for a variety of items as carbon taxes or other mechanisms are deployed.

- A number of industries that depend on underlying natural assets that are being adversely affected by a changing climate (or broader environmental degradation) may become unviable. Examples include alpine sports, coral coast tourism plus agriculture / aquaculture in certain regions.

- Additionally, businesses whose core activities are carbon intensive or otherwise environmentally degrading will face additional risks including:

  - Increased regulation, which in some cases may impact the organisation's license to operate;

  - Decreasing demand for products or services;

  - Damage to reputation; and

  - Difficulty or increasing costs to obtain finance.

Part 2 – Opportunity

- Conversely, a great deal of business opportunity lies ahead, with a variety of products and services needed to help societies adapt to the impacts of a changing climate.

- The associated change in societal attitudes will also stimulate demand for new products and services that can demonstrate superior "environmental performance" and may displace traditional alternatives in many sectors including transport, construction and energy.

- Potential opportunity areas are summarised in Table 12.

Part 3 – Preparing Your Business

- Currently, many corporate sustainability programs are superficial bolt-ons aiming to appeal to market and employee sentiment. They are typically not closely aligned with business strategy, in most cases falling well short of the greenhouse emissions reduction trajectories that are needed to avert significant climate change, and often ignore the growing risks associated with the changing climate, let alone considering the opportunities arising from adaptation.

Impact	Innovation / Opportunity
Increasing frequency & intensity of extreme weather (storm, flooding, drought, heatwave, bushfire, etc.)	• Storm/waste water infrastructure expansion / improvements • Flood defenses including portable systems for residential use • Disaster early warning services such as Aeeris • Fire retardant gel to protect buildings in the path of bush fires • Services to emergency services & post-disaster • Products to improve health & safety of outdoor workers (plus crops & livestock) • Healthcare
Climatic shift – warmer average temperatures & changes in precipitation affecting water supplies & agriculture; ocean acidification / de-oxygenation	• Genetic modification (drought/heat tolerance; pest resistance) • Agricultural advisory (crop & land use optimisation) • Water rights trading, desalination, pipe-laying & pumping • Fish farming (vegetarian species, filter feeders) • Air conditioning; medicines to reduce risk of heat stroke • Border protection / defense of food & water assets

Regulation – imposition of carbon prices and/or restrictions on fossil fuel use or other high emitting activities	• Fossil fuel & high emissions substitutes and offsets including:
	  • Renewable energy / carbon capture & storage / afforestation / reforestation
	  • Electric vehicles / charging infrastructure; high speed rail
	  • Energy efficiency (lighting, heating, cooling, ventilation, tri-generation, insulation, vehicles, etc.)
	  • Structural timber versus concrete/steel for high rise construction
	  • Biofuels (where land use makes sense)

Societal change – consumer / voter desire for products & services with lower environmental impact and better "corporate citizenry"	• Environmental remediation services (including e.g. minimisation of agricultural run-off) • Product / process redesign services, materials substitution, etc. • Eco-Labelling services • Legal services (class actions against polluters, etc.) • Socially responsible investments including fossil-fuel free funds • Risk management consultancy (reputational)
Sea level rise	• Coastal protection, beach renourishment • Infrastructure relocation / protection (ports, airports, transport corridors, cities) • Legal representation for & against councils and state governments versus coastal property owners

Table 12 – A range of business opportunities

• In response, the AdaptiveCMM assessment tool, considers the full breadth of capabilities an organisation needs to consider itself ready for the Adaptive Economy, namely:

- Effective governance, policy, decision-making and accountability around its strategy, activities and environmental consequences;
- Comprehensive measurement of its environmental impact, including up and down its value chain;
- Systematic, long term risk assessment that explicitly considers the disruptions anticipated from climate change;
- Resilience at strategic, cultural and operational levels;
- An action plan to reduce and ultimately negate its environmental impact;
- Stakeholder leadership on environmental matters, supporting and encouraging its broader community; and
- High levels of adaptive capacity, helping ensure the company produces the right products, the right way, at the right time for the right markets.

Having spent the first half of my career working in a variety of property, technology and risk management project roles for major corporates, I founded Adaptive Capability as a means of continuing to play to my strengths as a business consultant while having a sense of giving something back to the community, the environment and my family.

We are in the business of helping transform our clients' businesses for the mutual benefit of them, the environment, and a society that will be slightly better prepared for the impacts of climate change. While we're continually improving, my colleagues and I think of our business as an early example of what the Adaptive Economy is all about.

Some companies will lack the capacity to come to terms with the Adaptive Economy. They will become collateral damage of the disruptive shift caused by climate change and the crescendo of related innovation and change.

But spare a thought for the millions of individuals, predominantly in developing countries, who will be hardest hit by the effects of climate change. For example, those living in exposed low-lying coastal zones or islands, whose fresh water supplies and agricultural productivity are being compromised by the encroaching oceans as sea levels rise and violent storm surges push ever further inland. Or those whose livelihood depends on scratching a living from declining fisheries or parched fields. Or those in impoverished manufacturing centres such as Dhaka, Bangladesh, who will lose their jobs as companies in the developed world realize that the supply risks of continuing to deal with such a climate exposed country are becoming too great.

At the end of the day it comes down to a simple question: what sort of company do you want to be?

- ☑ One that enables customers and investors to feel a genuine sense of social responsibility through engagement with your organisation?

- ☑ One that demonstrates resilience and a stewardship approach with regards to limited natural resources?

- ☑ One whose actions pass the "front page of the newspaper" test for ethical and moral standards?

- ☑ One whose financial health will thrive during the 21st century?

or

- ☒ One that may run out of raw materials or be hit by excessive cost increases?

- ☒ One whose operations are routinely disrupted by extreme weather events?

- ☒ One that is losing its social right to operate and may in time lose its regulatory license?

- ☒ One whose revenues and market value will decline due to its failure to transform?

When put in these terms it's not such a difficult decision to make. The key is to make a conscious commitment to join the ranks of companies that will make up the Adaptive Economy. Start your journey today.

Acknowledgements

Writing a book is a journey that invariably involves making sacrifices. In particular I would like to thank my wife Felicity and children Charles and James for their support and perseverance in letting me undertake this project.

Thank you to my business partner Rod Crowder for his enthusiasm and encouragement; Dr Gary Buttriss for his invaluable advice during the development of the ACMM; my editor Willow Aliento, whose subject matter expertise proved invaluable; my sister Alison who volunteered to review the draft; and my graphic designer Michelle Lorimer.

I've appreciated learning from hundreds of sources in the research process and thank the many people and organisations whose work I have drawn on. A special shout to the climate science fraternity (and I use the word in its genderless form) whose patience and perseverance in uncovering the facts of anthropogenic warming and its impacts and communicating its findings to an often defensive audience is to be applauded and celebrated.

Finally a thank you to my parents, who brought me up to value the sustainable coexistence of business and humanity with the environment.

References

i. http://www.theguardian.com/environment/climate-consensus-97-per-cent/2014/may/23/john-oliver-best-climate-debate-ever

ii. www.skepticalscience.com

iii. http://en.wikipedia.org/wiki/Stephen_Emmott / 10 Billion book

iv. http://www.ipcc.ch/pdf/assessment-report/ar5/wg1/WG1AR5_SPM_FINAL.pdf

v. http://www.bp.com/content/dam/bp/pdf/Energy-economics/statistical-review-2014/BP-statistical-review-of-world-energy-2014-full-report.pdf

vi. https://flowcharts.llnl.gov/content/energy/energy_archive/energy_flow_2011/LLNLUSEnergy2011.png

vii. http://aodproject.net/news/58-time-for-super-funds-to-face-up-to-climate-risks.html

viii. http://www.epa.gov/climatechange/ghgemissions/global.html

ix. http://www.fao.org/forestry/30515/en/

x. http://www.researchgate.net/publication/228756550_Carbon_Dioxide_Emissions_from_the_Global_Cement_Industry_1

xi. http://www.ted.com/talks/hans_rosling_on_global_population_growth?language=en

xii. http://comres.co.uk/poll/1249/eciu-climate-change-poll-august-2014.htm

xiii. http://www.carbonbrief.org/blog/2014/09/polling-finds-conservative-mps-have-doubts-about-climate-science/

xiv. http://www.smh.com.au/business/markets/paris-un-climate-conference-2015-climate-deal-requires-23-trillion-investment-20151213-glmgs5.html

xv. CO2now.org/Current-CO2-Now/global-carbon-emissions.html

xvi. https://www.wickedproblems.com/1_wicked_problems.php

xvii. Climate Smart Development https://openknowledge.worldbank.org/bitstream/handle/10986/18815/889080WP0v10RE0Smart0Development0Ma.pdf?sequence=1

xviii. http://www.ipcc.ch/report/ar5/wg2/

xix. http://riskybusiness.org/uploads/files/RiskyBusiness_PrintedReport_FINAL_WEB_OPTIMIZED.pdf

xx. http://ase.tufts.edu/cosmos/view_chapter.asp?id=21&page=1

xxi. http://co2now.org/

xxii. http://www.c2es.org/facts-figures/main-ghgs

xxiii. http://people.exeter.ac.uk/TWDavies/energy_conversion/Calculation%20of%20CO2%20emissions%20from%20fuels.htm

xxiv. http://www.pbl.nl/en/publications/2012/trends-in-global-co2-emissions-2012-report

xxv. http://www.esrl.noaa.gov/research/themes/carbon/

xxvi. http://en.wikipedia.org/wiki/Temperature_record

xxvii. https://www2.ucar.edu/climate/faq/what-average-global-temperature-now

xxviii. http://environment.nationalgeographic.com.au/environment/global-warming/gw-overview/

xxix. http://www.education.noaa.gov/Weather_and_Atmosphere/Weather_Systems_and_Patterns.html

xxx. http://www.washingtonpost.com/news/energy-environment/wp/2015/03/23/global-warming-is-now-slowing-down-the-circulation-of-the-oceans-with-potentially-dire-consequences/

xxxi. http://time.com/3691920/climate-change-iceland/

xxxii. http://legal-planet.org/2011/07/19/frogs-boiling-water-and-climate-change-for-the-record

xxxiii. http://insideclimatenews.org/news/20140923/can-humanity-rise-climate-challenge

xxxiv. Source: http://tamino.files.wordpress.com/2012/11/bytype.jpg

xxxv.   Ernst & Young produced a useful report on stranded assets which you can find here http://www.ey.com/au/en/services/specialty-services/climate-change-and-sustainability-services/ey-lets-talk-sustainability-issue-4-stranded-assets-from-fact-to-fiction

xxxvi. http://www.abc.net.au/radionational/programs/bushtelegraph/alpine-tourism/5023908

xxxvii. http://www.gbrmpa.gov.au/__data/assets/pdf_file/0006/66417/Economic-contribution-of-the-Great-Barrier-Reef-2013.pdf

xxxviii. http://www.theguardian.com/environment/2015/jul/15/climate-change-costing-airlines-millions-of-dollars-in-extra-fuel-and-flying-time

xxxix. http://index.gain.org/

xl.   www.aphref.aph.gov.au-house-committee-ccea-ccbio-report-firstinterimreport-chapter4.pdf

xli.   http://www.berlindailysun.com/index.php?option=com_content&view=article&id=49621:snowmobiling-must-adapt-to-climate-change&catid=103:local-news&Itemid=442

xlii.   E. Chang, Journal of Transport Geography 2000 http://202.114.89.60/resource/pdf/2120.pdf

xliii. http://www.bbc.com/news/business-30393690

xliv.   http://unfccc.int/cooperation_and_support/financial_mechanism/green_climate_fund/items/5869.php

xlv.   http://www.climate-kic.org/

xlvi.   http://fs-unep-centre.org/publications/gtr-2014 & http://www.ceres.org/issues/clean-trillion/realizing-the-clean-trillion-progress-and-challenges/clean-energy-a-multi-trillion-dollar-opportunity-1

xlvii. http://www.iea.org/Textbase/npsum/EEMR2014SUM.pdf

xlviii. Figure SPM.2, in: Summary for Policymakers, p.7, in: IPCC AR5 WG3 (2014), Edenhofer, O., et al., ed., Climate Change 2014: Mitigation of Climate Change. Contribution of Working Group III (WG3) to the Fifth Assessment Report (AR5) of the Intergovernmental Panel on Climate Change (IPCC), Cambridge University Press.

xlix.   http://www.ft.com/cms/s/0/962714b6-4611-11e2-ae8d-00144feabdc0.html#axzz3ky07YH2M

l.   http://www.mooreslaw.org/

li.   Gartner estimates the ICT industry accounts for approximately 2% of Global anthropogenic carbon emissions: http://www.gartner.com/newsroom/id/503867

lii.   http://www.epa.gov/climateleadership/documents/supplier_profiles.pdf

liii.   http://tasmaniantimes.com/index.php/article/cape-grims-new-detections

liv.   https://www.ipcc.ch/pdf/special-reports/srren/SRREN_FD_SPM_final.pdf

lv.   http://www.solarroadways.com/

lvi.   http://reneweconomy.com.au/2014/deutsche-bank-sees-50-us-states-solar-grid-parity-2016

lvii.   http://www.hydroworld.com/articles/2014/12/eu-report-listing-us-1-6-trillion-investment-opportunities-may-spur-hydropower-development.html

lviii.   www.teslamotors.com/about/press/releases/nevada-selected-official-site-tesla-battery-gigafactory

lix.   http://www.cityofsydney.nsw.gov.au/vision/sustainable-sydney-2030

lx.   http://www.economist.com/news/science-and-technology/21600656-thorium-element-named-after-norse-god-thunder-may-soon-contribute

lxi.   http://www.forbes.com/sites/williampentland/2014/10/15/lockheed-martin-claims-fusion-breakthrough-that-could-change-world-forever/

lxii.   http://www.nature.com/news/us-government-abandons-carbon-capture-demonstration-1.16868

lxiii.   http://ecomento.com/guide/hydrogen-fuel-cell-vs-battery-electric-cars-greener/

lxiv.   http://www.skeptical science.com/Graphene-SkS.html

lxv.   www.mpoweruk.com/energy_efficiency.htm and www.eia.gov/tools/
          faqs/faq.cfm?id=105&t=3

lxvi.   www.fueleconomy.gov/feg/evtech.shtml

lxvii.   http://media.wix.com/
          ugd/7a1536_0c0ebc3ec1a24f7fb73b0e5668ca974e.pdf

lxviii.   http://www.traveller.com.au/planes-v-fast-trains-tortoise-
          and-the-air-1c6hh

lxix.   http://www.greenbiz.com/article/tommies-2014-best-bio-
          inspired-designs

lxx.   http://www.nytimes.com/2015/02/17/world/americas/drought-
          pushes-sao-paulo-brazil-toward-water-crisis.html?_r=0

lxxi.   http://www.abc.net.au/science/articles/2013/12/06/3906589.htm

lxxii.   http://www.pub.gov.sg/water/newater/Pages/default.aspx

lxxiii.   http://www.smh.com.au/environment/water-issues/toilettotap-
          recycled-water-gets-the-hard-sell-20130309-2fsnp.html

lxxiv.   An atmospheric water generator http://www.skywell.com/

lxxv.   http://pacinst.org/publication/bottled-water-and-
          energy-a-fact-sheet/

lxxvi.   http://water.epa.gov/infrastructure/sustain/energyefficiency.cfm

lxxvii.   http://www.bbc.com/news/business-19661006

lxxviii. http://www.mq.edu.au/pubstatic/public/download.jsp?id=131844

lxxix.   http://www.epa.sa.gov.au/environmental_info/container_deposits

lxxx.   http://www.smh.com.au/environment/litter-data-recycles-case-for-
          bottle-and-can-refund-20130410-2hlty.html

lxxxi.   See The Sixth Extinction by Elizabeth Kolbert http://www.pulitzer.org/
          works/2015-General-Nonfiction

lxxxii.   Derived from http://www.ext.colostate.edu/mg/
          gardennotes/720.html

lxxxiii. http://www.epa.gov/climatechange/impacts-adaptation/
          agriculture.html

lxxxiv. http://www.theage.com.au/victoria/diet-change-cuts-methane-emissions-in-cow-burps-20150804-girf6l.html

lxxxv. http://www.technologyreview.com/featuredstory/522596/why-we-will-need-genetically-modified-foods/

lxxxvi. Derived from http://faostat.fao.org/site/377/DesktopDefault.aspx?PageID=377#ancor: total land area 13,009,101.8 (x1000ha); all agriculture 4,922,206.6 of which all pasture 3,359,658.6; forest 4,021,910.8; other uses 4,074,444.5.

lxxxvii. http://www.theguardian.com/science/2013/aug/05/synthetic-meat-burger-stem-cells

lxxxviii. http://www.smh.com.au/environment/climate-change/hotter-harder-times-forecast-for-the-farm-as-climate-changes-food-production-20150314-143xai.html

lxxxix. http://www.smh.com.au/environment/climate-change/hotter-harder-times-forecast-for-the-farm-as-climate-changes-food-production-20150314-143xai.html

xc. http://www.canberratimes.com.au/act-news/human-waste-is-a-safe-fertiliser-expert-20130701-2p5wz.html

xci. http://phys.org/news/2012-06-genetic-alternative-fertilizer.html

xcii. http://science.time.com/2012/04/26/whole-food-blues-why-organic-agriculture-may-not-be-so-sustainable/

xciii. www.carbonfarmersofaustralia.com.au/About/what-is-carbon-farming

xciv. http://rstb.royalsocietypublishing.org/content/365/1554/3065.short#conclusions

xcv. http://www.theguardian.com/sustainable-business/2014/oct/17/tackle-food-waste-global-consumption-conundrum

xcvi. http://www.woolworths.com.au/wps/wcm/connect/webSite/Woolworths/about+us/woolworths-news/woolworths+launches+local+food+sourcing+strategy

xcvii. http://www.mistra.org/en/mistra/news/news-archive/2014-05-09-mistra-supports-large-scale-algaculture-on-west-coast.html xcviii. Angel et al 2005 cited by: http://www.fao.org/docrep/010/ag049e/AG049E03.htm

xcix. http://landscapeperformance.org/case-study-briefs/cheonggyecheon-stream-restoration

c. https://blogs.csiro.au/climate-response/stories/greening-urban-areas-can-help-reduce-future-impacts-of-heatwaves/

ci. City if Sydney for example e.g. http://www.cityofsydney.nsw.gov.au/vision/towards-2030/sustainability/carbon-reduction/urban-heat-island],

cii. http://www.canadiangardening.com/how-to/pests-and-diseases/how-air-pollution-affects-plants/a/41680

ciii. http://ntrs.nasa.gov/archive/nasa/casi.ntrs.nasa.gov/19930073077.pdf

civ. switchboard.nrdc.org/blogs/kbenfield/us_home_size_preferences_final.html

cv. www.planning.nsw.gov.au/Portals/0/DeliveringHomes/Planning_Granny_Flats_Generalinformation.pdf

cvi. http://www.thefifthestate.com.au/innovation/design/the-three-principles-of-sustainable-home-cooling/71507

cvii. http://www.themonitor.com/building-foundations-crack-as-texas-drought-shifts-soil/article_65b7af4d-eead-5154-9edc-e69db453b451.html

cviii. http://www.rblandmark.com/News/Articles/6-10-2014/Farmers-Insurance-drops-suit-against-villages/

cix. http://www.theguardian.com/world/2014/jul/11/miami-drowning-climate-change-deniers-sea-levels-rising

cx. https://www.wickedproblems.com/1_changing_workforce.php; originating from www.conecomm.com

cxi. http://www.un.org/en/events/desertificationday/background.shtml

cxii. Hot: Living Through the Next Fifty Years on Earth http://markhertsgaard.com/hot-living-through-the-next-fifty-years-on-earth/

cxiii.   www.unilever.com.au/innovation/productinnovations/
           coolicecreaminnovations/

cxiv.   http://citiscope.org/story/2014/can-app-borrowing-housewares-
           make-neighborhoods-stronger.

cxv.   David Ranson https://theconversation.com/death-in-a-hot-climate-
           southern-heatwave-to-take-its-toll-22039

cxvi.   http://www.floodcommission.qld.gov.au/__data/assets/pdf_
           file/0003/8787/QFCI-Interim-Report-Chapter-6-Essential-services.pdf

cxvii.   For example http://www.csiro.au/Outcomes/Climate/Understanding/
           State-of-the-Climate-2012/Temperature.aspx

cxviii.   http://www.livescience.com/13296-european-russia-heat-waves-
           climate-change.html

cxix.   http://www.theguardian.com/environment/southern-
           crossroads/2014/jan/17/heat-wave-australia-record-breaking-climate-
           change-bushfires-melbourne

cxx.   http://startup88.com/hardware/2014/09/10/5-things-sexy-new-
           apple-watch-cant-cant/8379

cxxi.   https://www.whitehouse.gov/the-press-office/2015/04/07/fact-sheet-
           administration-announces-actions-protect-communities-impacts-

cxxii.   http://m.smh.com.au/environment/climate-change/sweating-it-out-
           climate-change-extremes-to-impact-on-sport-20150130-1328cq.html

cxxiii.   http://www.nytimes.com/2015/02/20/us/battle-rises-in-florida-keys-
           over-fighting-mosquitoes-with-mosquitoes.html?_r=0

cxxiv.   http://www.nytimes.com/2013/03/03/opinion/sunday/friedman-the-
           scary-hidden-stressor.html?_r=0

cxxv.   http://www.scribd.com/doc/242845848/Read-DoD-report-2014-
           Climate-Change-Adaptation-Roadmap

cxxvi.   http://www.sustainalytics.com/sites/default/files/water_in_china-_
           issues_for_responsible_investors_feb2010.pdf

cxxvii.   http://www.washingtonpost.com/politics/obama-to-create-worlds-
           largest-protected-marine-reserve-in-pacific-ocean/2014/09/24/
           e2ecaab4-433e-11e4-b47c-f5889e061e5f_story.html

cxxviii. eg http://www.pwc.com/gx/en/capital-projects-infrastructure/chinas-infrastructure-investment-in-africa.jhtml

cxxix. http://www.lawyersweekly.com.au/news/11210-bushfires-spark-liability-debate

cxxx. http://www.100resilientcities.org/blog/entry/what-is-a-chief-resilience-officer1#/-_/

cxxxi. http://www.forbes.com/sites/petercohan/2013/02/26/4-reasons-marissa-mayers-no-at-home-work-policy-is-an-epic-fail/

cxxxii. ciencemag.org/content/early/2015/01/14/science.1259855.abstract

cxxxiii. http://www.smh.com.au/world/eight-million-tonnes-of-plastic-added-to-ocean-every-year-study-20150212-13d9da.html

cxxxiv. http://www.invenzone.com/research_papers/recovery-of-materials-from-waste-printed-circuit-boards-by-vacuum-pyrolysis-and-vacuum-centrifugal-separation-60250501

cxxxv. http://www.water.nsw.gov.au/ArticleDocuments/34/recovery_hn-nutrient-export-monitoring-farm-runoff-managing-nutrient-pollution.pdf.aspx

cxxxvi. http://www.miningaustralia.com.au/features/what-should-we-do-with-australia-s-50-000-abandone

cxxxvii. http://www.postmining.org/our-work/current/101-things/index.php / http://www.smh.com.au/business/pressures-on-coal-show-no-signs-of-ending-20141228-12enrk.html

cxxxviii. http://www.theguardian.com/environment/2011/aug/23/species-earth-estimate-scientists

cxxxix. http://www.iflscience.com/plants-and-animals/current-extinction-rate-10-times-worse-previously-thought

cxl. https://theconversation.com/the-mercury-level-in-your-tuna-is-getting-higher-37147

cxli. http://news.nationalgeographic.com/news/2015/02/150210-national-academy-geoengineering-report-climate-change-environment/

cxlii. http://www.bbc.com/news/science-environment-30543252

cxliii.   http://www.theguardian.com/environment/2013/jan/22/mineral-dust-oceans-carbon-geoengineering

cxliv.   http://www.footprintnetwork.org/en/index.php/GFN/page/world_footprint/

cxlv.   http://www.radionz.co.nz/news/national/262551/study-puts-price-tag-on-dairy

cxlvi.   http://thinkprogress.org/climate/2014/11/12/3591433/china-renewable-energy-commitment/

cxlvii.   http://www.environment.gov.au/climate-change/carbon-neutral/ncos

cxlviii.   http://www.sei.cmu.edu/reports/01mm001.pdf

cxlix.   https://www.globalreporting.org/reporting/g4/Pages/default.aspx

cl.   http://www.fsc.org.au/downloads/file/ResearchReportsFile/2011_0725_ESGREPORTINGGUIDEPRINTandPOSTPROOFVersion.pdf

cli.   http://www.sbr-online.de/pdfarchive/einzelne_pdf/sbr_2013_july_312-329.pdf

clii.   http://faculty.babson.edu/krollag/org_site/org_theory/march_articles/cohen_abcap.html - original publication,

cliii.   https://www.gmo.com/docs/default-source/research-and-commentary/strategies/asset-allocation/the-world's-dumbest-idea.pdf

cliv.   http://www.foodstandards.gov.au/consumer/labelling/ingredients/Pages/default.aspx

clv.   For example Citigroup, as reported in the New York Times http://dealbook.nytimes.com/2013/05/23/banks-lobbyists-help-in-drafting-financial-bills/?_r=0

clvi.   http://reneweconomy.com.au/2015/fossil-free-stock-indices-outperformed-benchmarks-us-australia-91825

clvii.   http://www3.weforum.org/docs/WEF_Global_Risks_2015_Report15.pdf

clviii.　http://www.mercer.com/content/dam/mercer/attachments/global/
investments/responsible-investment/Climate-change-scenarios-
Implications-for-strategic-asset-allocation.pdf

clix.　http://www.isa.org.usyd.edu.au/

clx.　http://www.wri.org/sites/default/files/WRI13-
IPCCinfographic-FINAL_web.png

clxi.　http://www.ibm.com/annualreport/2014/bin/assets/IBM-Report-of-
Financials-2014.pdf

clxii.　http://recyclingnearyou.com.au/cartridges/

clxiii.　http://www.nabers.gov.au/public/WebPages/DocumentHandler.
ashx?docType=3&id=115&attId

Select Bibliography

Conway, Erik M. & Orsekes, Naomi, *Merchandes of Doubt*, Bloomsbury Publishing, 2010.

Diamond, Jared, *Collapse: How Societies Choose to Fail or Succeed*, Penguin / Viking, 2005.

Dietz, Rob & O'Neill, Dan, *Enough is Enough: Building a Sustainable Economy in a World of Finite Resources*, Routledge, 2013.

Emmott, Stephen, *10 Billion*, Penguin, 2013.

Flannery, Tim, *The Weather Makers: How Man Is Changing the Climate and What It Means for Life on Earth*, Grove Press, 2015.

Funk, McKenzie, *Windfall, The Booming Business of Global Warming*, Penguin, 2014.

Gladwell, Malcolm, *David and Goliath: Underdogs, Misfits and the Art of Battling Giants*, Hachette Book Group, 2013.

Hertsgaard, Mark, *Hot: Living Through the Next Fifty Years on Earth*, Mariner, 2011.

Juniper, Tony, *What Has Nature Ever Done for Us: How Money Really Does Grow on Trees*, Profile Books, 2013.

Klein, Naomi, *This Changes Everything*, Penguin, 2015.

Marshall, George, *Don't Even Think About It: Why Our Brains Are Wired to Ignore Climate Change*, Bloomsbury, 2014.

McKibben, Bill, *Eaarth: Making a Life on a Tough New Planet*, Times Books, 2010.

Pearse, Guy, *Greenwash, Big Brands and Carbon Scams*, Black Inc, 2012.

Senge, Peter (et al), *The Necessary Revolution: How Individuals and Organizations are Working Together to Create a Sustainable World*, Nicholas Brealey Publishing, 2008.

Slade, Giles, *Climate Chnage and the Coming Fight for Survival*, New Society Publishers, 2013.

Index

About the Author

David McEwen is founder and Director of Adaptive Capability, a strategic management consultancy advising business on risks and opportunities related to climate change and other macro environmental issues. He is focused on how we will need to redefine our relationship with nature and reshape our buildings, cities, companies, energy systems, transport infrastructures, food and water sources and societies in the coming decades to meet these growing challenges.

David has had a 20 year consulting career, assisting clients in a range of countries and industries on a variety of issues. He also worked for the New Zealand Treasury. Coming from an environmentally conscious family, he began developing consulting services around the theme of corporate sustainability and energy efficiency about ten years ago.

A New Zealander, he currently resides in Sydney, Australia with his wife and two children. He holds a Master of Business Administration from the Australian Graduate School of Management and was winner of the AGSM Alumni Association Prize. This is his first book.

www.ingramcontent.com/pod-product-compliance
Lightning Source LLC
Chambersburg PA
CBHW070351200326

41518CB00012B/2207